Grace Does That?

Grace Does That?

The Surprising Power of God's Amazing Grace

Perry Hall

MORGANTOWN, KY 42261

Copyright © 2020 by Perry Hall

All rights reserved. No part of this book may be reproduced, stored in a retrieval system, or transmitted in any form or by any means-electronic, mechanical, photocopying, recording, or otherwise, without written permission from the publisher.

Unless otherwise noted Scripture quotations taken from the New American Standard Bible® (NASB), Copyright © 1960, 1962, 1963, 1968, 1971, 1972, 1973, 1975, 1977, 1995 by The Lockman Foundation. Used by permission. www.Lockman.org.

ISBNS: 978-1-948696-26-5 (Paperback), 978-1-948696-23-4 (Hardback), 978-1-948696-19-7 (Kindle)

Library of Congress Control Number: 2020946446

Cover images licensed through Canva
Cover created in Canva

Printed in the United States of America

TOLE PUBLISHING, PO BOX 1098,
MORGANTOWN, KY 42261-8411

www.tolepublishing.com

I Dedicate This Book to My Parents

Mom, from you I have gained a greater desire to be like you because you show a great love for people. When I reach out to others, it is often because of the tireless example you have shown to me. My desire to be like you has been an influence in my life for good. Because of you, you have unknowingly helped many people through me. I admire you greatly Mom. My heart is from you.

Dad, from you I have gained a greater desire to be like you because you show a great desire for learning. When I strive for truth and understanding, when I endeavor to work hard, when I value great intellect, and when I have the ability to teach others with effect, it is because of the good example you have shown to me. I admire you greatly Dad. My head is from you. Because of you two I feel and think. Because of you two I can serve with both my heart and my head. Because of you two I am who I am.

Contents

	Warning Label	ix
	Preface	1
1.	The Grace That Builds Confidence	5
2.	The Grace That Is Sufficient	26
3.	The Grace That Is Understood	46
4.	The Grace That Obligates	83
5.	The Grace That Motivates	111
6.	The Grace That Rekindles	137
7.	The Grace That Worships	171
	Conclusion	193
	Bibliography	194
	Acknowledgements	197

Warning Label

"Sarcasm Ahead!" Sarcasm, but it is not the searing, sardonic, and scathing kind that fills the pages of this book. My sarcasm is more facetious and fun than hurtful or spiteful. I prefer to think of it as witty, not withering. Sarcasm can often make a point quickly and clearly.

"Silliness Ahead!" Along with sarcasm, there is a lot of silliness. Humor is how I communicate. I see a lot of humor in the Bible. Humor is a uniquely human characteristic. Being created in the image of God, I think God has a sense of humor—just look at the platypus! So, amid the amusing anecdotes, and silly illustrations, there are serious points.

"Seriousness Ahead!" While hopefully, my writing style is "an easy read," scriptures will be delved into deeply but discussed plainly. This being a verse-by-verse study, context will show us the writer's mind in a way otherwise impossible. This book is for both those in the pews and in the pulpits. The seriousness is revealed in respecting the author's flow of thought, our own self-examination, and the amazing awe-struck enlightenment in realizing we are discussing God's grace.

"Scriptures Ahead!" God's words are far more important than ours. You will find most of my scripture references to be full quotes. Why? I assume you are a lot like me—I do not look up all the references listed in books and articles. So to help emphasize God's words, I put the actual Biblical texts from "The Book" into my book. So try not to skip over the scriptures . . . because that is something I would never do! (Self-deprecating sarcasm intended.)

PERRY HALL

I hope my sarcastic, silly style does not offend. If it does, I hope you discover this only after you have paid for my book! (Sarcasm intended.)

Preface

Grace.

Can a topic be both overexposed yet underdeveloped? Yes! That is the paradoxical premise of this study. Yes, grace is a gift, but it is a gift that keeps on giving because it is also a tool for every day living. As you read this book, I hope that you will think with pleasant surprise, "Grace does that?"

Considering the Originator of grace, we should expect to never exhaust our learning about this grand topic because we cannot exhaust our learning about the Grace Giver. We should expect grace to be deeper than the ocean God created, higher than the expanse of space, and more multifaceted than the most precious jewels.

To illustrate, let's compare grace to a diamond. How many purposes are there for diamonds?—simply put, what's a diamond good for?

- It is used as a cutting tool, even as a surgical instrument
- It is used as a tool or abrasive
- It is turned to powder or paste for grinding and polishing
- It was used as needles on record players

Additionally, all those uses don't even touch on the most obvious use of a diamond—to bribe women to marry us men—and to make up for our mistakes after they marry us! The surprising number of functions of diamonds is indisputable and impressive.

The more we learn about diamonds, the more uses we see that they have, and the more impressed we are about them. In fact, the more we learn about the uses of diamonds, the more lessons we learn about purposes still unknown and undiscovered. Similarly, the more we learn about grace, the more uses we discover it has, the more impressed we are with God's grace, and hopefully, we will begin wondering what other new truths God can reveal to us about His amazing grace.

So what can grace do? That's what this book is about. Grace can give us the confidence to approach God (Heb. 4), motivate us beyond our natural ability and common sensibility (2 Cor. 8–9), obligate us to obedience (Rom. 6), cause us to be fruitful through a better and deeper understanding of Christ (Col. 1), rekindle our fire of faith (2 Tim. 1–2), cause us to burst out in worshipful song (Col. 3), sustain us through disappointing times—including when we are disappointed with God (2 Cor. 12), and vastly more. I did not even mention the most common thing grace can do, which is to save us (Eph. 2:8). Grace is not only received, it is used. Grace is not only theological, it is practical. Grace is to be used in speech, in worship, and in life.

All of the above and even more is expressed by a phrase found in 1 Peter 4:10, "As each one has received a special gift, employ it in serving one another as good stewards of the manifold grace of God." Manifold (*poikilos*) means "many-colored," "various," or "varied." Doesn't that fit the analogy of a diamond perfectly?

In this book, how are we going to see the different dimensions, uses, and manifold purposes of grace? Simple. We are going to discover how the New Testament uses grace in context—context will be our prism, our diamond loupe, our microscope, and diamond tester. This is not a topical study of grace, but rather an expository look at grace. We are going to look at grace the way one looks at a diamond, up close and personal. Simply put, this book will examine what the Holy Spirit reveals through various texts to see how and why the inspired writers used the precious jewel of grace. What lessons were Bible writers, through the Holy Spirit, trying to teach?

Let me share a bit of personal history with you. I do not remember what prompted this expository approach to the study of grace, but I do remember what it was not—I didn't begin my study in order to write a book. In recounting the beginning of this series of studies, my wife said she couldn't remember what sparked this approach either, but she did remember my effervescent response. After making a list of the occurrences of grace within the New Covenant, I systematically started studying one at a time within its context, letting the inspired text form my conclusions. What my wife remembers about this period was the excitement with which I came home after each study proclaiming, "Guess what I learned about grace today!" My reaction explains the title, *Grace Does That?*

Grace. Are you ready to go digging for something greater than diamonds? Let's see what God has to say about His grace. Let's see how grace "graces" our lives every day. Grace does that? Yes! Grace does that!

1

The Grace That Builds Confidence

Hebrews 4.14–16

Once upon a time in the 1980s, the date? Well, I can't remember exactly. I've slept since then, but I certainly remember it was 6:30 in the morning when I heard a knocking at the door. At that time of the morning, it had to be important, right? An old lady—emphasize old—asked me, a stranger, if she could borrow my phone. Of course, I let her in, thinking it must be an emergency. After all, I was a stranger. Because of her impaired eyesight, she asked me to look up a number for her in the phone book and then dial it, which I did. Poor thing . . . all this trouble to make a phone call . . . at 6:30 AM . . . at a stranger's house . . . it had to be important, right?

Walking out of the room to give this lady some privacy, I was still close enough to hear the very first words that came out of her mouth, "I was in town and just thought I'd call to say hi."

I guess it didn't have to be important, did it?

Why did this stranger confidently knock on the door of an unknown person at 6:30 AM and ask to use the phone? Possibly, it was because she knew a preacher lived there, and therefore, it was not only safe but permitted, maybe even expected. The other likely reason was . . . well, this was Caneyville,

Kentucky, population 650. There are just some things you can do in a small town that you can't do any place else.

Knocking on the spiritual door of heaven (Matt. 7.7-8) with full confidence that the door will be opened is a blessing Christians enjoy by grace, even if we only want to just say hi. "Therefore let us draw near with confidence to the throne of grace, so that we may receive mercy and find grace to help in time of need" (Heb. 4.16). But as we see from this verse, Jesus is there when it is important, too, isn't He?

But pay close attention. If we view this verse only from a twenty-first-century Christian perspective, from the comfortable confines of our common religion, we will miss the wallop on their first-century religious reality. The shock comes if we view this verse from the Old Testament perspective of these New Testament "Messianic Jews." Remember, the book of Hebrews was written to . . . Hebrews.

The whole point of Hebrews is about approaching God, about sinful humans being sin-free so that we can approach the sinless Father of the Sin-bearer. Grace allows us to draw near in order to find grace and mercy—and we can do this confidently.

In William Barclay's introduction to Hebrews, he describes four distinct, yet proper biblical conceptions of religion: (1) an inward fellowship with God; (2) a standard for life and a power to reach that standard; (3) the highest satisfaction of their minds; and (4) access to God (Barclay 1–2). Maybe a practical way to describe these four purposes is:

1. *Spiritually personal.* Often we have heard the phrase, "Accept Jesus as your personal Savior." There is nothing more personal than being saved, and Jesus saves us one by one. Kittel, surveying pre New Testament usage of *mathetes* (disciple), discusses two competing notions of the disciple/teacher relationship among the Greeks (Theological Dictionary of the New Testament (TDNT), Vol. 4, 416ff). The one we are concerned with here is the one describing a New Testament disciple: one who lives like his teacher. The predominant idea pictures a disciple as one who "imitates his teacher and focuses on the personal relationship between the two."

2. *Spiritually practical.* Some viewing religion this way might say, "I am a better husband, father, friend, neighbor, and person because of Jesus." Shouldn't believers be changed and challenged by their spirituality? As an example, consider the following anecdote:

> An outspoken atheist in the early part of this century, Charles Bradlaugh, challenged a preacher named Hugh Price Hughes to a public debate in London. The preacher gladly accepted the challenge, but on one condition. He wanted to bring one hundred men and women to the debate who would be witnesses for the redeeming love of God. These men and women would demonstrate for unbelievers how God had turned their lives around. The preacher asked his atheist challenger to do the same thing: to bring one hundred people whose lives were helped by not believing in God. The debate never took place. The atheists never showed up. (Moore, 6–7)

3. *Spiritually intellectual.* The Bible is the one book that if we ever stop studying because of boredom, we had actually stopped studying long before that point without even realizing it. It is filled with simple truths that lead to paradoxes of life. It is filled with truths about the infinite God, so how could we who are finite ever finish studying it? More and more, I am convinced that in the Bible, we not only see the mind of God in what is revealed but also in how it is revealed. Christianity is spiritually and intellectually stimulating .

4. *Spiritually approachable.* This is what we are focusing on here. God, Jesus, and the Holy Spirit are always there for us. We can approach the throne of grace without fear of rejection. We know that the Almighty hears our prayers . . . because of grace.

Before examining Hebrews 4.16, let's back up to chapter one to help us grasp the mental shock that comes from being able to approach Jesus—no that isn't strong enough—from being able to boldly and confidently approach Jesus on His throne of grace.

Have you ever been told, "You just don't get it?" Whether said in frustration or spite, the meaning usually is, "You're not very bright." Sometimes our "brightness" can shine through if we simply change the direction of our thinking. After all, even a flashlight isn't very bright when turned flush against the wall.

Well, there is a chance when studying Hebrews that we just don't get it! I'm not trying to be insulting. We just need to change our perspective—I know I had to. We can't look at Hebrews through twenty-first-century Gentile eyes. We have to become Jewish in our mindset. We have to think like a people who had worshipped with fear for over a millennium. We have to think like a people who had their high priest go into the Holy of Holies once a year wearing bells (Ex. 28.33–35) and a rope around his ankle. Why? To drag out the dead body; if the other priests stopped hearing the rattling of the bells, they would assume the high priest was dead. Why would the high priest be dead? Because God had struck him dead for irreverence while in His presence. While the high priest wearing a rope around his ankle might be apocryphal, it at least illustrates the mindset that perpetuated the story—FEAR! "It shall be on Aaron when he ministers, and its tinkling shall be heard when he enters and leaves the holy place before the LORD, so that he will not die." (Ex. 28.35) We have to think like a people who have "come to a mountain that can be touched and to a blazing fire, and to darkness and gloom and whirlwind, and to the blast of a trumpet and the sound of words which sound was such that those who heard begged that no further word be spoken to them. For they could not bear the command, 'if even a beast touches the mountain, it will be stoned.' And so terrible was the sight, that Moses said, 'I am full of fear and trembling.'" (Heb. 12.18–21).

Let's begin our mind-bending, enlightening exercise in chapter 1 of Hebrews because we cannot appreciate Hebrews 4.16 unless we first comprehend the staggering truth of who the Jewish Jesus is!

And He is the radiance of His glory and the exact representation of His nature, and upholds all things by the word of His power. When He had made purification of sins, He sat down at the right hand of the Majesty on high. Hebrews 1.3

By grasping the awesomeness that Jesus is "the radiance of His [i.e., God's] glory" (Heb. 1.3), we gain some Jewish insight into He who sits on the throne of grace whom we can confidently approach in prayer. To the Jewish mind, Jesus being "the radiance of God's glory" meant much more than that Jesus is "The Light" (John 1.4). I am not trying to "dim" the importance of John's concept. Not at all, but there is a history that "illuminates" the Hebrew expression far brighter than simply "light." John probably spoke against the background of gnostic illumination. I would not darken the understanding that John's phrase is filled with a brightness of its own, just as bright, but different than in Jewish thought. However, to not see the Jewish history of the radiance of God's glory might be comparable to not seeing the difference between the brightness of a light bulb and the sun. Listen to a self-described Messianic Jew:

> "The radiance of His glory" is best rendered Jewishly as the Sh'khinah, which the Encyclopedia Judaica (Volume 14,1349–1351) defines as: "The Divine Presence, the numinous immanence of God in the world . . . a revelation of the holy in the midst of the profane. . . ."

Now, mentally retrieve the purpose of Hebrews— "let us draw near." The author continues:

> One of the more prominent images associated with the Shekhinah is that of light. Thus, on the verse, ". . . the earth did shine with His glory" (Ezekiel 43.2), the rabbis remark, 'This is the face of the Shekhinah' (Avot diRabbi Natan [18b–19a]; see also Chullin 59b–60a). Both the angels in heaven and the righteous in olam ha-ba ("the world to come") are sustained by the radiance of the Shekhinah (Exodus Rabbah 32.4, B'rakhot 17a; cf. Exodus 34.29-35). . . .

According to Saadiah Gaon [882–942 C.E.], the Shekhinah is identical with *kevod ha-Shem* ("the glory of God"), which served as an intermediary between God and man during the prophetic experience. He suggests that the "glory of God" is the biblical term, and Shekhinah is the Talmudic term for the created splendor of light, which acts as an intermediary between God and man, and which sometimes takes on human form. Thus when Moses asked to see the glory of God, he was shown the Shekhinah, and when the prophets in their visions saw God in human likeness, what they actually saw was not

God Himself but the *Shekhinah* (see Saadiah's interpretation of Ezekiel 1.26, 1 Kings 22.19, and Daniel 7.9 in Book of Beliefs and Opinions 2.10).

The point of these citations is not to suggest that Yeshua is a "created splendor of light," but to convey some of the associations of the expression, "the brightness of the glory" or the radiance of the *Sh'khinah*. (Stern, 662–663)

So Jesus being the Shekinah means He was the presence of God among men. This is more than Him being Jewish. This sounds like the incarnation. In Hebrews 1.3, we have Jesus being the temple of God in the flesh (Jn.2.14–22).

Let's skip ahead just a second. Jesus was the presence of God among men, and when we approach the throne of grace, when we approach Jesus, we are approaching God. From a Jewish perspective, that is shocking! To see God in the Old Testament brought death (Judg. 13.22). Yet, we are called to confidently approach God the Son on the throne of grace.

Another point worth noting is that since Jesus is the radiance of God, or the Shekinah of God, following Jesus was and is very Jewish—even their Hebrew fathers unknowingly were following Jesus. Jesus preexisted before His incarnation as the cloud or light of God's glory on earth. This had to be comforting to these first-century Messianic Jews. They hadn't abandoned their heritage after all.

Once I was speaking with a friend of mine who happened to be a Reformed Jew. He was telling me of an experience he had with a non-Jewish rabbi. He was the rabbi of a temple of "Messianic Jews" who are Jews by culture, heritage, and race, yet believe that Jesus is the promised Jewish (and Gentile) Messiah. The Reformed Jew said he had never heard of anything like that, but then admitted, even though he was Jewish, he has always believed Jesus was God. He reasoned, "Who else could He have been?" And yet, he was still surprised that Jews actually and openly professed this view.

Jewish Christians. Whoever heard of such a thing? I told him that all Christians, in the beginning, were Jews. Even Jesus Christ was Jewish. And according to Romans 2.29, we are all Jewish!

When thinking of Jesus as the radiance of God's glory, think of Mt. Sinai where Yahweh spoke to the nation of Israel: "And to the eyes of the sons of

Israel the appearance of the glory of the LORD was like a consuming fire on the mountain top" (Ex. 24.17).

When thinking of Jesus as the radiance of God's glory, think of God's presence filling the tabernacle: "Then the cloud covered the tent of meeting, and the glory of the LORD filled the tabernacle" (Ex. 40.34).

When thinking of Jesus as the radiance of God's glory, think of Yahweh's approval of His temple: "Now when Solomon had finished praying, fire came down from heaven and consumed the burnt offering and the sacrifices, and the glory of the LORD filled the house. The priests could not enter into the house of the LORD because the glory of the LORD filled the LORD'S house. All the sons of Israel, seeing the fire come down and the glory of the LORD upon the house, bowed down on the pavement with their faces to the ground, and they worshiped and gave praise to the LORD, saying, 'Truly He is good, truly His lovingkindness is everlasting' " (2 Chron. 7.1–3).

When thinking of Jesus, think of God! When thinking of Jesus, the Jews needed to remember the Shema (a Heb. term for a prayer that incorporates the core belief of Judaism): "Hear, O Israel! The LORD is our God, the LORD is one! (Deut. 6.4). When the Jews could do this, that's when they got it! Do we? This is Who we boldly come before in prayer. Can we grasp the awesomeness both for Jewish Christians and Gentile Christians?

Let us get back to our text about approaching God on His throne of grace.

Hebrews 4.16 begins with "therefore." As they say, "When you see a therefore, see what it is there for." Well, what proceeded the therefore of 4.16? There are actually five "therefore's" in just chapter 4! Please read each one.

4.1: "Therefore, let us fear if, while a promise remains of entering His rest, any one of you may seem to have come short of it."

4.6: "Therefore, since it remains for some to enter it, and those who formerly had good news preached to them failed to enter because of disobedience."

4.11: "Therefore let us be diligent to enter that rest, so that no one will fall, through following the same example of disobedience."

4.14: "Therefore, since we have a great high priest who has passed through the heavens, Jesus the Son of God, let us hold fast our confession."

4.16: "Therefore let us draw near with confidence to the throne of grace, so that we may receive mercy and find grace to help in time of need."

Therefore, I suggest that therefore is therefore important and is there, therefore, for a reason! Sorry . . . couldn't resist! Now, seriously, let's go back to the first therefore (4.1) in this chapter because we cannot afford to miss what they missed out on.

Let's look at fear for a moment. Fear is going to be mixed with confidence. Christianity is filled with paradoxes. We fear God, but we also fear not being with God. But in the above verse, notice that the fear here is not of God. The fear is of missing out on being with God. What a profound difference! The Old Covenant Israelites feared coming into the presence of God. The New Covenant Jewish Christians should fear not being in the presence of the same God. And neither should we Gentile Christians.

Yet, there is a proper place for the fear of God, even for us. The context of fear is connected to both obedience and punishment (Heb. 3.7ff). It is important to keep fear in its context and in a healthy attitude. Biblical fear of God does not come from the unknown, but the known. It is not a fear of ill will. It is not a fear of flippant judgment. It is not a fear of masochistic derangement. As my father said, "God is not a 'gotcha' God." The real fear of the faithful comes when we cannot be in God's presence.

Fear can be used in many ways. This same word (*phobeo*) is used of Moses and his birth family not fearing Pharaoh (Heb. 11.23) and of believers not fearing people due to their relationship with God (Heb. 13.6).

Fear can be rational or irrational, right or wrong, and terrorizing or reverential. I find it intriguing that the use of fear in Hebrews 4.1 is tied to something positive instead of negative—although scripture uses fear in the opposite way also. Even though the result would be the same—not receiving the promise—the emphasis is on what we would lose and not on the punishment. Think about that. Do we emphasize not going to hell more than going to heaven? If God offered us an alternative choice, annihilation, instead of hell or heaven, would we consider that a viable and appealing offer? Would we choose ceasing to exist so that we could live all of our earthly life however we desired? I guess what I am asking is, are we more interested in spending an eternity with God, or not spending an eternity in hell? When thinking of everlasting damnation, do we comprehend that the ultimate punishment is not being cast into fire, but being cast away from the presence of God? The only reason the outer darkness exists is because it is away from the God of Light and from Jesus, the radiance of His glory.

Does missing out on spending time with God terrify us? Hebrews 4 teaches there is a rest promised. That rest is still future, but there is rest for us every time we approach the throne of grace. I have confidence mixed with reverential fear because I fear not being with God.

Rest. What a comfortable word. Do you ever get tired? Are you ever spiritually exhausted? Do you ever wish Jesus would come back as quickly as possible? With me, the answer is yes . . . sometimes. Why? Because here in this life, I am unable to completely and fully rest. Yes, I know Jesus promised rest; "Take My yoke upon you and learn from Me, for I am gentle and humble in heart; and you will find rest for your souls. For My yoke is easy, and my burden is light" (Matt. 11.29-30). That is rest that results from forgiveness. That rest is based upon realizing we don't have to prove ourselves worthy—we are sharing Jesus' yoke. But we are still in a spiritual battle today. Jesus never granted us rest from living in a sinful world. He never promised us perpetual rest from temptation. That's why we need to go to the throne of grace promised in verse 16. Going to the throne, talking to Jesus is our comfort and our rest.

Yes, we get tired. Even Jesus got tired, at least physically, and maybe emotionally. Why do you think He prayed so often? Prayer—approaching the throne—brings us rest as it did Jesus. Our mind and spirit enter into God's presence. Our mind transcends this world's problems and enters into the other world's solutions. When Jesus prayed, His mind and spirit entered into God's presence.

We all get tired. What's so dangerous about being tired?

Getting tired can make us want to rest, but not at the foot of the throne of grace. When we get tired, should we also get terrified? After all, the wandering Israelites must have gotten tired, and they failed.

3.12–13: "Take care, brethren, that there not be in any one of you an evil, unbelieving heart that falls away from the living God. But encourage one another day after day, as long as it is still called 'Today,' so that none of you will be hardened by the deceitfulness of sin."

Yes. Get terrified! Why? I am going to let you in on a little secret, but you probably already know this. When I get tired, my real self is oftentimes revealed even more glaringly. Has that ever happened to you? When I get tired, I can't hide, especially since:

4.12–13: "The word of God is living and active and sharper than any two-edged sword, and piercing as far as the division of soul and spirit, of both joints and marrow, and able to judge the thoughts and intentions of the heart. And there is no creature hidden from His sight, but all things are open and laid bare to the eyes of Him with whom we have to do."

Yes. Be terrified…unless we are approaching the throne of grace in our time of need.

Being tired and wanting to rest is a natural desire that can make us follow the Israelites example of disobedience and quit. The Israelites quit on God. Three times the Hebrew writer records God's lament: "they shall not enter my rest" (3.11; 4.3,5). Be fearful of not entering into our rest. That healthy fear will cause us to go to the throne of grace in our time of need.

"But wait," you might be thinking, "grace means I cannot fall!" Not according to Hebrews. Grace means when I start to fall, God will lift me up… if I approach the throne of grace. Grace is a gift to keep me from falling. Grace is my confidence.

You might be wondering, "But doesn't that cause us to fear losing our salvation?" Change your focus! What it should cause us to fear is losing out on being with God, of entering our rest. Living in grace, we never lose our salvation. Giving up on grace is giving up on God.

So remember, there is a difference between resting and quitting. Jesus was made like unto us in all things. He was tempted in that which He suffered. He left His place of rest in order to become tired, weary, and exhausted. But because He never quit, this enables Him to be the perfect High Priest.

4.14: "Therefore, since we have a great high priest who has passed through the heavens, Jesus the Son of God, let us hold fast our confession."

Quick question: what is the only New Testament book that teaches us that Jesus is our High Priest? If you are surprised that there is only one, you and I are in the same company.

> [Hebrews] is the only place in the N.T. where we have a full-scale treatment of our Lord's high priestly ministry in heaven. . . . It is unique in its wonderful contribution on the eternal finality of our Lord Jesus as Sinbearer, High Priest, and Sanctifier of His people. (Baxter, 388)

Our Priest sits on a throne! Our Sacrifice has mercy to give grace and authority to give grace. Our Jesus did something greater than passing through the man-made veil of the temple and tabernacle. Our High Priest passed through the heavens. Here is an: "Allusion to the high priest of the Old Covenant, who, in order to make atonement for the people, passed through the courts of the Temple, and through the Temple itself, into the Most Holy Place" (Meyer, 492). "Through, and up to the throne of God of which he wields the power, and is thus able to fulfill for his followers the divine promise of rest" (Vincent in Meyer, 430).

After passing through created heavens, Jesus then went through the greater and more perfect tabernacle, not made with hands, that is to say, not of this creation (Heb. 9.11). More on that is found in chapter nine of Hebrews.

Entering into heaven and serving as High Priest, Jesus has entered into His rest. Entering into His rest, Jesus has ceased living among the temptations of the flesh. Imagine the daily torture for Him while "tabernacling" in the flesh on earth (2 Pet. 2.7–8). No wonder He often approached the throne in prayer.

The Hebrew writer in 4.14 then calls our High Priest and King by His human name (Jesus) and His divine name (Son of God). In doing this, the writer hints back to chapter 1, where he proved Christ's divinity and chapter 2, where he emphasized Jesus' humanity.

The exhortation "let us hold fast" (4.14) means "to cling to tenaciously" (Robertson, vol.5, 365). We have a saying that illustrates this idea: "to hold on for dear life."

Never before had I experienced that grip of life and death until riding a carnival ride with my first child. Round and round we went for fun—except that the attendant had not checked my child's safety belt, which came undone. Screaming at the controller . . . bracing my knee against the metal side . . . and simultaneously holding my daughter in place with my arm . . . unconcerned for my own life—teaches me that I must spiritually hold fast as much as I physically held fast to my child. Life is at stake — eternal life.

The whole book of Hebrews is encouraging us to enter our rest and to approach the throne of grace. The whole book is about not failing, not falling, and not quitting. The whole book is about approaching the throne of grace. Grace is not just for the fallen. Grace is for those wanting to stand . . . while on their knees.

We are to hold fast our confession. Our confession which we hold fast, concerns the Jewish and Gentile Messiah and our relationship to Him. We are confessing Him whom we can fearlessly approach on His throne of grace. This confession is more than not being embarrassed to pray out in public when at a restaurant. We need to go back and see this through their first-century lives. Jewish Christians were to live a life of confession both in harmony with their physical heritage and spiritual inheritance.

Why should we hold fast our confession? Next verse, please. . . .

4.15: "For we do not have a high priest who cannot sympathize with our weaknesses, but One who has been tempted in all things as we are, yet without sin."

Earlier I mentioned being tired of this world, and I am sure I share this feeling with others in the faith. But, we cannot give up, even though we have weaknesses. We must press on like many others who have come before us, and yet, we must be unlike those who have fallen by the wayside. Diligence is ever needed (v. 11). Thankfully, gracefully, this verse is not just about me and you and our weaknesses. It is also about He who now sits on the throne of grace. We are to find comfort in that which we cannot fully understand—Jesus incarnate.

What I am about to ask and say needs careful consideration. It is impossible to explain what we have never experienced, and none of us have experienced being in the form of God and taking the form of bond-servant and being found in the likeness of man (Phil. 2.6–7). Which brings to mind a serious question: is it a denial of omniscience to believe some knowledge is only obtained empirically? To answer "no" does not deny the omniscience of God, and it might help us better understand why Jesus needed to become our High Priest. Is it possible Jesus needed to live as a man not only for us but also for Deity? I don't know. Let me repeat that. I don't know. But could it be possible that God the Father "cannot sympathize with our weaknesses" (Heb. 4.15) because He didn't become flesh? Yet, Jesus can sympathize with our weaknesses. Why? Because He experienced humanity and was "tempted in all things as we are, yet without sin" (Heb. 4.15). Could there be a difference in knowledge in understanding man that comes from being man, rather than from creating man? Jesus also learned obedience (Heb. 5.8). Isn't this learning by experience? And would not this verse, by implication, reach back before the incarnation to when Jesus submitted to the Father to become the Son of man? Before becoming man, could He sympathize with man as a man? Wisdom is the proper use of knowledge. Some knowledge is empirical, such as living as a man. We have a High Priest who understands us. Here is how someone else explained it: "This is more than knowledge of human infirmity. It is feeling it by reason of a common experience with men" (Vincent in Meyer, 430).

Because my High Priest can sympathize with me, I unflinchingly approach His throne of grace. Jesus can sympathize because He was tempted in all things. Again, this is a topic beyond personal experience: how can God be tempted? Whether we are ever able to grasp the temptation of Jesus, there is one thing of which we are certain: He was yet without sin!

The fact that Jesus was without sin means that he knew depths and tensions and assaults of temptation, which we never can know. So far, from his battle being easier, it was immeasurably harder. Why? For this reason—we fall to temptation long before the tempter has put out the whole of his power. We never know temptation at it fiercest because we fall long before that state is reached. But Jesus was tempted far beyond what we are, for in his case, the tempter put everything he possessed into the assault. Think of this in terms of pain. There is a degree of pain which the human frame can stand—and when that degree is passed, a person loses consciousness so that there are agonies of pain he cannot know. It is so with temptation. We collapse in (the) face of temptation, but Jesus went to our limit of temptation and far beyond it and still did not collapse. It is true to say that he was tempted in all things as we are, but it is also true to say that no one was tempted as he was. (Barclay, 42)

This again gives me the bravery and confidence needed. He never quit God. He rested in God.

4.16: "Therefore let us draw near with confidence to the throne of grace, so that we may receive mercy and find grace to help in time of need."

Wow! What a long journey to see what the "therefore" was there for. Because we need help, because others have failed, because Jesus is the Son of God, because He understands, because He was tempted, because He didn't fail, because whatever trouble you and I currently are in, therefore let us draw near (7.25; 10.19-22). "This verb in Hebrews means reverent approach for worship" (Robertson, vol.5, 366). Confidence does not exclude reverence.

We draw near with confidence. The Century Dictionary gives "confidence" three definitions. Which do you think best fits the type of confidence we have in Jesus in this verse?

1. Reliance on one's own powers, resources, or circumstances; belief in one's own competency; self-reliance; assurance.

2. That in which trust is placed, ground of trust; that which gives assurance of safety, security.

3. Boldness; courage; disregard or defiance of danger.

If I didn't know the answer, I would guess the second—trust. But that would be wrong. Hebrews uses the word "faith" to convey that kind of confidence. In this verse, the word for confidence is *parrhesia*. What is this confidence? This word has other translations within the NASB that shed some light on the meaning: publicly, plainly, openly, boldness, openness. It is all-out freedom of speech. It is assurance, unreserved utterance. It is the absence of fear in speaking and in living, hence, confidence, cheerful courage, and boldness. It is walking into the holy of holies without fear of being struck dead.

10.19: "Therefore, brethren, since we have confidence to enter the holy place by the blood of Jesus."

Confidence or boldness is a paradoxical trait when coupled with meekness. But remember that we are meek when looking at ourselves and confident when looking to our Lord. Jesus is our confidence, our hope. This confidence is not a defiant cockiness, but rather an absence of the fear of rejection. Our petitions might be rejected because God does not always say "yes." But we will not be rejected. And when God says "no," we are confident that He is not saying "no" to us personally, but rather to our requests.

What do we have to hold fast to? Our confidence and the boast of our hope. Both words, confidence and boast, are related to our speech. This is how we talk; we speak confidently. Rejoicing, we speak. We approach the throne of grace speaking with confidence because we are living with confidence in the grace of God.

I have tried to connect Hebrews 4.16 with the whole Hebraic message. Hopefully, you do not feel we have been wandering in the desert for 40 years looking for the connection!

We draw near with confidence to the throne of grace. That glorious phrase is found only here in the entire Bible. Our High Priest is also our King. The throne of grace is equivalent to the mercy seat found in the Tabernacle and Temple.

If we need forgiveness, we need to know the throne, which is founded upon righteousness—a righteousness that justly condemns us but is also able to disperse grace. What's the difference between grace and mercy? Mercy is not receiving what we should; grace is receiving what we should not. Mercy is God's pitying love; grace is God's gift of love. Another possible difference is that mercy is given when we fail to combat temptation, and grace is given to combat the temptation. Grace is a very practical gift from God. Of that, I am confident.

Let's contemplate what the implications are concerning the throne of grace. As stated before, this is the only time this phrase is used in the entire Bible. If I am correct in what I am about to say, the implications are even greater to the Jewish mind than at first sight. I believe the throne of grace is the mercy seat. Even more than that, I wonder if Jesus is the throne of grace Himself.

Our time of need is the time we can approach God—confidently approach— without fear. Is this your time of need? Not once a year, as with the Jews on the Day of Atonement, which was the only time the high priest could approach the mercy seat. We can confidently, without fear, boldly approach the throne, anytime, anywhere, because of grace. That's a door we can knock on and be let in, not to a stranger's house, but to our God's house. Go ahead, knock on the door, confidently. To Jesus, we are that important.

Questions

1. Name the four spiritual practical purposes of religion:

_____

_____

_____

_____

2. In Hebrews 1.3, Jesus is described as the "radiance of God's glory". As they thought back to God's glory in the wilderness, what was the Jewish word that the Hebrew Christians associate as the meaning of this phrase?

_____

_____

3. How would having a Hebrew mindset of the fearsomeness of God's glory have shocked these Jewish Christians? How does knowing this help our concept of "approaching the throne of Grace with boldness? Hebrews 4.16

_____

_____

4. When thinking of Jesus as "the radiance of God's glory", name the four ways we should think of Jesus:

_____

_____

5. How can knowing the four ways we should think of Jesus from the Hebrews point of view help us in our understanding of Jesus and the confidence we should have to receive mercy and grace?

_____

_____

_____

_____

6. Hebrews 4.16 begins with a "therefore". Where are the five preceding "therefore(s) in Hebrews 4 and to what do they pertain?

_____

_____

7. What should be feared as mentioned in Hebrews 4.1? How does this switch of fear of being in the presence of God as the Hebrews of old to this new fear give us confidence to approach the "throne of grace"?

_____

_____

8. Having "fear" of God is proper, as He is God. What are some unhealthy unbiblical ways to fear God? What are some healthy biblical ways?

_____

_____

_____

9. What is the ultimate punishment of hell? How does knowing this give enlightenment to better confidence in approaching the "throne of grace"?

_____

_____

10. Hebrews 4 speaks of a "rest" promised. What are some things we should receive "rest" from spiritually when we become Christians? What are some things we will not receive "rest" from until we pass from this life?

_____

_____

_____

11. How can becoming physically tired become a cause of sin? How can approaching the throne of grace with confidence in our time of need combat this?

_____

_____

_____

12. How is resting and having confidence in grace different than "quitting" and doing whatever we want?

_____

_____

13. Where in the New Testament can we find that Jesus is our High Priest?

_____

14. Hebrews 4.14 tells us to "hold fast" our confession of Jesus as the Son of God and our High Priest who passed through the heavens. How does this help us have confidence? (See Hebrews 4.15)

_____

_____

15. How should knowing Jesus lived as a man give us confidence in his sympathy with our weaknesses?

_____

_____

16. What are the seven reasons for the "therefore(s) as listed near the end of this chapter?

_____

_____

_____

_____

_____

_____

_____

17. In Hebrews 4.16 the word "boldness" or "confidence" is used which comes from the Greek word *parrhesia*. What does this word mean and how can this increase our confidence when approaching the throne of grace?

_____

_____

18. What is the difference between "grace" and "mercy"? How can knowing we have a "throne of grace" to approach give us confidence?

_____

_____

2

The Grace That Is Sufficient

2 Corinthians 12 (go ahead and read chapters 10–13)

Besides salvation, what first-century gift would you choose? Would you want to perform miracles? I have always thought that would be awesome. How about being directly inspired by God? It would be nice to know I was always right when I preached! Would you want to be an apostle? That would be the big one, wouldn't it? With it, you get everything—miracles, inspiration, and authority. Paul received that very special gift of grace and all the pain that came with it.

Now let's look at the text....

12.1: "Boasting is necessary, though it is not profitable; but I will go on to visions and revelations of the Lord."

Paul's "boasting" goes back to chapter 11, his "*corona muralis*." What's that? I didn't know either until a friend asked me if I thought Paul was referring to it. Not wanting to admit my intellectual weakness, I didn't reply to him until after I found out!

So what is the *corona muralis*? Roman soldiers received the prestigious "mural crown" by successfully being the first person to scale the besieged enemy's wall. That took guts ... or stupidity. Paul scaled the wall—backwards, down it, and out of the city—escaping, not conquering, allowing himself to suffer weakness by hiding in a basket like a coward ... so that God could use him for strength (11.32–33). That stuttering sentence is hard to read, but Paul's escape wasn't easy either. Obviously, Paul's "boasting" was not the Corinthians' boasting.

Boasting about his weaknesses, Paul chastises both the Corinthians and the false apostles by getting down on their level and "playing their game" (2 Cor. 11). With sarcasm dripping from his pen, he listed some of his special "qualifications," which I believe explains his thorn in the flesh (2 Cor. 11.22–33):

> Are they servants of Christ?—I speak as if insane—I more so; in far more labors, in far more imprisonments, beaten times without number, often in danger of death. Five times I received from the Jews thirty-nine lashes. Three times I was beaten with rods, once I was stoned, three times I was shipwrecked, a night and a day I have spent in the deep. I have been on frequent journeys, in dangers from rivers, dangers from robbers, dangers from my countrymen, dangers from the Gentiles, dangers in the city, dangers in the wilderness, dangers on the sea, dangers among false brethren; I have been in labor and hardship, through many sleepless nights, in hunger and thirst, often without food, in cold and exposure. (2 Corinthians 11.23–27)

That's boasting? That's how people normally brag? No. That is sarcasm. Can we all agree that Paul does not just say things without reason or for shock value? Understanding that, we still might be a little surprised that 2 Corinthians contains little sarcastic phrases that Paul uses—not to hurt—but to teach (11.8, 11.19).

Sometimes—and sadly—sarcasm is the only method left. The intention is to quickly punch and then proceed. Paul defends himself with sarcasm and foolishness. His qualifications were his persecutions. Could the "super-apostles" (12.11, alternate translation) say that? Being filled with grace does not mean we are milquetoast Christians, allowing others to insult and walk all over us. Paul defends himself but not for self-glory. Paul defends himself for God.

After discussing his thorn, his boastings, Paul continues by listing his truly special qualification—and this time with seriousness and humility. Continuing in chapter 12, he includes his visions and revelations, which were further signs of his apostleship . . . and God's grace.

In some ways, 2 Corinthians is the most personal and pitiful epistle written by Paul. By pitiful, I do not mean badly written, but rather that it is pitiful that it needed to be written. Some things shouldn't need saying and doing. Sadly, Paul is forced to defend himself through his boasting and his apostleship to the very people who should have believed in him the most.

STOP! Right there, right where Paul is . . . can you empathize with Paul? "Right there" is a place we have all stood. "Right there" is a kind of "weakness" that has to be dealt with right now. "Right there"…maybe "right here"…is where we need to remember that our ultimate confidence, our ultimate sufficiency, is not found in what others think of us. It is found in God and in His grace.

Paul's second letter is an unfortunate, heartbreaking book. Previously, in 1 Corinthians 9.2, he had written, "If to others I am not an apostle, at least I am to you; for you are the seal of my apostleship in the Lord." Can you hear the pain in his pen? Others didn't believe in him, but at least the Corinthians were on his side. However, in the second letter to the Corinthians, he has to answer their personal attacks, including their attacks on his apostleship (2 Cor. 11.5–6). Doubt replaces confidence. Those who "had his back" now backed away.

STOP! Haven't we all stood where Paul stood? Haven't we all faced criticism not only personally, but in our service to God? Paul is not alone. We are not alone. We need to do exactly what Paul is about to do—speak of grace, and remember God's grace is sufficient.

12.2-4: "I know a man in Christ who fourteen years ago—whether in the body I do not know, or out of the body I do not know, God knows—such a man was caught up to the third heaven. And I know how such a man—whether in the body or apart from the body I do not know,

God knows—was caught up into Paradise and heard inexpressible words, which a man is not permitted to speak."

Don't you wish we knew more about what happened to Paul? Sometimes we just don't know everything we want to. Three of my favorite words are, "I don't know." We have to be content in not being filled in by God. Sometimes, not having the answers to everything is exactly where God wants us to be. Frustrating isn't it? Remember when we get frustrated . . . God's grace is sufficient. We don't need to know everything we want to know. We just need to know Him who knows everything.

Trying to distance himself from the false apostles who commended themselves (10.12), Paul speaks in the third person. Just think, for 14 years, Paul kept this glorious vision to himself. He must have been pretty good at keeping secrets and equally good at not bragging and boasting about himself. That's a lesson we all could learn better! That's a lesson his opponents never grasped.

Paul humbly talks about his experience in such indirect terms to possibly magnify the gift and not himself. Perhaps, the false apostles also claimed visions and revelations, but nothing like this. Paul's humility would be a marked contrast to the self-promoting, posturing, fake apostles. Humility is also a gift of grace.

Historically, two men—Enoch and Elijah—were caught up into heaven without first dying. Their bodies, I assume, were changed. But no one else had ever had an experience like Paul—he is caught up, but comes back! Up there in paradise, he heard inexpressible words, which a man is not permitted to speak. Now the sarcastic is mixed with the oxymoronic: inexpressible words. Sarcasm, oxymorons, and paradoxes. Paul is pulling out imaginative methods trying to reach the hearts of the people he loves even though they are the source of his pain.

12.5: "On behalf of such a man I will boast; but on my own behalf I will not boast, except in regard to my weaknesses."

Contrast Paul's attitude with that of many of us who find it too easy to show off using God's gift. As a silly illustration, let me say that not once, not even a little bit, have my tools burst out bragging. Yes, there are different levels of tools, but even the best tool in the wrong hand (e.g., mine) is inferior to the worst tool in a skilled hand. We all are inclined to be "talking tools." But not Paul. While we are good at verbally giving God the credit, do we sometimes mentally brag on ourselves? Just a little? Pride is foolish; it is like a shovel taking credit for digging a deep hole, or a saw for cutting a straight line. Don't be a talking tool!

As an example of someone who did not feel the need to brag on his position in the local congregation, an elder suggested the following for the leadership page of their church web site (wschurch.com):

> Leadership: Jesus Christ—Owner, Reports directly to God.
>
> Born in a barn in or near Bethlehem, Judea, He was raised by working-class parents in Nazareth after a brief stay in Egypt. He was educated in the synagogue, and worked in skilled trades as a young man.
>
> Although He was not known for his good looks, He amazed the local religious leaders with his knowledge and teaching. He further amazed the general populace with His ability to control nature, heal the sick, and raise the dead. He offered Himself in payment of the penalty for our sins against God worthy of death.
>
> Although resisting temptation and living a perfect life, He was executed like a common criminal outside of Jerusalem by the Roman occupation forces. He now rules in Heaven as High Priest, King, and Intercessor for those who are willing to acknowledge their sin, repent, be baptized for remission of their sins, and become committed to his cause of redemption and reconciliation to God. Those who accede to his rule are known as Christians. He is our leader, and we are his servants.

Isn't it refreshing and biblically sound for leaders to emphasize that they are in reality followers? "Boasting" that we are followers is better than boasting that we are leaders.

12.6: "For if I do wish to boast I will not be foolish, for I will be speaking the truth; but I refrain from this, so that no one will credit me with more than he sees in me or hears from me."

"'It ain't boastin' if it's true." Have you ever heard that? Still, this kind of boasting makes Paul uncomfortable, and yet he apparently has no choice. It is sad to be put in such an uncomfortable situation by those you trusted and still love.

12.7: "Because of the surpassing greatness of the revelations, for this reason, to keep me from exalting myself, there was given me a thorn in the flesh, a messenger of Satan to torment me—to keep me from exalting myself!"

Ahhh, the "the thorn in the flesh." Paul's thorn is a mystery too good to pass up, especially since it deals with "grace being sufficient." I have already stated what I believe it is—the apostleship and trouble associated with it. So why do I think that? Context. Try an experiment: read chapters 11 and 12, believing that you will find the answer to the riddle of the thorn, and you will. The key is discovering what Paul says is his "weakness" (11.30; 12.5,9,10; 13.4).

Paul's thorn: what do we know about it, just from this verse? It's always good to start with definitions so let's begin with "thorn" (*skolops*):

1. "This old word is used for splinter, stake, thorn. In the papyri and inscriptions examples occur both for splinter and thorn as the meaning. In the LXX, it is usually thorn." (Robertson, IV, 265.)

2. "It is a stake for a palisade, or for impaling; a surgical instrument; the point of a fish-hook. In the Septuagint, it occurs three times, translated thorn in Hos. ii 6, where, however, it is distinguished from . . . thorns; brier in Ezek. xxviii.24, and prick in Num. xxxiii.55. Nine different Hebrew words are rendered by thorn, for which, in the great majority of cases, Septuagint gives [another word]. The rendering thorn . . . has no support. The figure is that of the impaling-stake." (Vincent, III, 354.)

3. In defining the word "cross," the ISBE says, "In the Greek language it is *stauros*, but sometimes we find the word *skolops* used as its Greek equivalent." (www.bible-history.com/isbe/C/CROSS/).

In looking at these definitions, maybe the common concept of a "thorn" is just not painful enough. Isn't there a huge difference, literally, between a splinter and a cross? Paul's thorn was painful.

We also learn that Paul's thorn was a blessing—a balance to keep Paul humble. Suffering and blessing are two words that don't seem to match—a paradox of Christianity. Herein is an axiom of spiritual life: the greater the blessing, the greater the possibility that the blessing can become a curse. (For example, would you object to inheriting a million dollars from a rich uncle? Could such a blessing be dangerous [1 Tim. 6]?) And yet, suffering to prevent sin is not a curse but a blessing, albeit disguised. Remember, a blessing can become a curse, and what appears to be a curse can be a blessing. Go ahead and reread that. It is a hard concept to understand, but the key to it is God's grace.

Another truth about Paul's situation is that both the vision and the thorn are related. This suffering is not due to Paul's unrighteousness, but to safeguard his righteousness. Paul might have responded to the thorn by saying, "Take the vision back!" After all, he did ask for the thorn to be taken away. Do you think he would have chosen the vision knowing he would receive a thorn as a means to balance the glory? Would we?

We also learn that the thorn in the flesh is the messenger of Satan to torment or buffet (KJV) him. To torment means "to strike with clenched hands" (Vine, 158).

> In the present subjunctive, we have the iterative idea of blows that are struck with the closed fist. This verb is rare, yet it is used three times in the New Testament, figuratively in 1 Cor. 4.11 and literally in Matt. 26.67 where the Sanhedrists beat Jesus after they had condemned him. Derived from the word for "knuckles," it means to strike with the fist so that the hard knuckles make the blow sting and crush. (Lenski, vol. 7, 1300)

Paul is not just inconvenienced, slapped, or harassed—that is not forceful enough. He is beaten. Remember that when interpreting Paul's thorn in the flesh (12,10). It is demeaning to Paul's situation, and to God's grace, to claim that our driving an old junker of a car is our thorn in the flesh, and our cross to bear (Luke 14.27). Paul suffered, and we suffer. Suffering is as real as happiness. Suffering is as real as grace.

And finally, we also learn that Satan is just as real as God. Never should we downplay the intelligence of Satan. I do not know if the devil can read my mind (he is not omniscient), but he knows me better than just about anyone else—sometimes even better than myself. He knew how to get to Paul, and he knew how to get Paul to plead for relief. He knows how to get to me, and he knows how to get to you.

12.8: "Concerning this I implored the Lord three times that it might leave me."

Paul asking and believing that Jesus could remove his suffering, shows his faith and confidence. Paul asking three times, shows his faith and perseverance. Paul asking no more, shows his faith and acceptance. Which is more spiritually challenging:

> Praying, believing that God can help?
> Continuing to pray, hoping God will help?
> Ceasing to pray, accepting that God is already helping?

Before focusing on Paul ceasing to pray, let's look at his asking. He implored (*parakaleo*) Jesus. This word means "I. to call to one's side, call for, summon ... II. to address, speak to, (call to, call one) ... 2. to beg, entreat, beseech" (Thayer, 482). It doesn't appear, therefore, that Paul was praying a casual prayer. Before we stop asking, let's make sure we are asking with the same intensity that Paul exemplified.

Paul prayed three times; Jesus prayed three times. Then both quit. I do not want to put a limit on how many times we can pray for a particular thing (Matt. 7.7–11). Yet, I believe that we should accept the first answer. However, I believe we are allowed to keep asking and hoping. Eventually, there comes a time when we must finally and resolutely accept God's answer and quit hoping He will change His mind, realizing His answer is best. That is difficult. I do not mean our ceasing to petition—although that might be hard—but accepting God's will as best. Accepting that God is helping us, just not in the way we prefer, is never easy. But accepting is more than just being resigned that things will not change. True Biblical acceptance is then glorifying God for His saying, "NO." That is harder than accepting, isn't it?

The "trick" to handling any suffering comes with our attitude. (1) "What can I learn from this?" (2) "How can I glorify God in this?" If we can turn suffering around, then we can endure it gladly ... dare I say, "graciously."

12.9: "And He has said to me, 'My grace is sufficient for you, for power is perfected in weakness.' Most gladly, therefore, I will rather boast about my weaknesses, so that the power of Christ may dwell in me."

My grace is sufficient for you. I find this phrase interesting. Usually, when we are suffering, we complain that we don't deserve our pain, despite the fact God promises us His grace to meet our needs. Read this next sentence slowly and let it sink it. Since none of us deserve God's grace, God is giving us what He says we don't deserve to balance that which we complain we don't deserve. Sounds ironic, doesn't it? Could we admit that this is another paradox of Christianity?

Look at the word sufficient (*arkeo*): "to be possessed of unfailing strength; to be strong, to suffice, to be enough (as against any danger; hence to defend, ward off" (Thayer, 73). Our English word just does not sound strong enough, does it? When I think of sufficient or adequate, I think of just barely enough. Our English word is not sufficient enough! Through a more thorough examination of this word, we find that it is related to the idea of raising a barrier (Strong's). Maybe the idea is that God's grace, Christ's strength, defends us against that which is attacking us. Yes, a good offense is sometimes needed, and we all need to be strong enough to wield the sword of God. But sometimes defense is all we need. Sometimes we simply (easier said than done) need to sit, be quiet, and endure the onslaught, knowing that God's wall of grace will keep the enemy out. That wall is high enough to get the job done. And yet just barely high enough means what to us? High enough. It is sufficient.

If this thorn in the flesh is what I believe it is, then Paul has it within his power to remove it—but not with the approval of God and not without severing His fellowship with God. Stay in grace and receive grace; or reject grace. Sounds like an easy decision when put that way, doesn't it?

Through suffering, God taught Paul that strength—maybe all strength—comes from weakness. Think: isn't it amazing that our most glaring weakness can become our biggest strength? That is the paradox of strength, weakness, and grace. That is the power of God. I am beginning to understand that most of Christianity is a paradox. The meek shall inherit the earth (Matt. 5.5). The last shall be first (Matt. 19.30). I can't live unless I die (Rom. 8.13). I can't be strong unless I am weak (2 Cor. 12.9). Even the meek Jesus, putting Himself last, died into order to live by allowing Himself to be weak and be consumed by weakness to display the power of God.

> For indeed He was crucified because of weakness, yet He lives because of the power of God. For we also are weak in Him, yet we will live with Him because of the power of God directed toward you. 2 Corinthians 13.4

When we accept God's answer, we are accepting His will and His grace. If we do not accept God's answer, we are declaring His grace is insufficient. Is anyone willing to shout that? Sometimes in our public prayers, the one praying will utter, "Not our will, but Thine be done," almost with a sigh, weakly resigning ourselves to God's will. How about also triumphantly saying, "Not our weakness, but your power!" And, "Not our will, but your grace be received!"

Deity answered Paul's prayer, but not the way Paul wanted. Remember, all prayers are answered. Jesus promised, "My grace is sufficient for you," and then He tells us why—for power is perfected in weakness. How is this done? How is power perfected in weakness? This is truly a paradox of life. If we supply a few words, then it will make sense: [God's] power is perfected in [my] weakness.

If I rely only upon my strength, certain things will happen. I will fail—sometime, somewhere, somehow. When I succeed, I will glory self and not God—until I fail, sometime, somewhere, somehow. Then I will blame God unless I am humbled—which is accepting weakness. When we hear some folks blow and brag, we are reminded of the time the flea said to the elephant, "Boy, didn't we shake that bridge when we crossed it?" Do we sometimes forget that God is the elephant, and we are the flea?

Here is a real-life example of the power in weakness that can come from unexpected places:

Jim Moore recalls when he visited a woman in the hospital who had lost her will to live:

> She had no cards or flowers, and she sat all day in a darkened room. But Jim was terrified. He felt that he was too inexperienced, and that he wouldn't know what to do. And his nervousness affected his visit. First, he pushed the door open too hard, and it slammed against the wall. Next, he walked over and accidentally kicked the bed. He stammered, stuttered, and said all the wrong things in between long periods of embarrassed silence. Finally, he tried to say a prayer, but even that didn't come out right. He left the room that day with tears in his eyes. He felt ashamed that this woman needed him, and he had failed her. But a few days later, Jim went courageously back. Imagine his surprise when he found the woman sitting up in bed writing letters. Flowers and cards were everywhere. She recognized him at once and began thanking him over and over for the visit he had paid her. Jim was confused because he knew he had botched the visit. He had done everything painfully wrong, and he confessed as much to her. "But that's just it," she replied. "I felt so sorry for you! It was the first time I had felt anything but self-pity for months. And that little spark of compassion for you gave me the will to live." (Moore, 96–98)

Strength can come from weakness because our weaknesses are often blessings in disguise. Although I do not believe that the weakness of which Paul speaks is a spiritual weakness, or a weakness of the flesh, or one that easily gives in to temptation, the same application can still be made. I can only overcome my spiritual weaknesses when:

> I recognize I have a weakness.
>
> I accept the fact that I cannot conquer my weakness.

Now, before I go any further, does that remind us of anything? Are you familiar with the Twelve Steps of Alcoholics Anonymous (AA)? The first one is, "We admitted we were powerless over our addiction—that our lives had become unmanageable." Bill W., the founder of AA, realized and publicized that the twelve steps came from the Bible. Recovery from any kind of weakness comes from relying on God's strength.

We cannot receive strength from God's grace until we put on His grace. Let's use armor as an analogy. What would you think of a knight who refused to put on his armor, believing his skin was tough enough? At worst, he is insane, at best, just plain stupid! Isn't the very fact that a knight who puts on armor is admitting weakness in order to put on strength? I cannot become stronger unless I accept I am weak.

Too often, though, we want to ignore the obvious. Listen to this fable by Aesop:

> A goatherd had sought to bring back a stray goat to his flock. He whistled and sounded his horn in vain; the straggler paid no attention to the summons. At last, the goatherd threw a stone, breaking the goat's horn. He begged it not to tell his master. The goat replied, "Why you silly fellow, the horn will speak though I be silent.

It is obvious that God is stronger than I; therefore, I should not attempt to hide things which cannot be hid. Instead, I should unleash the power of God, receive His grace, and be empowered to glorify Him.

After admitting our failures, problems, and inabilities, and then accepting and relying upon God's strength, we can now "boast." Boasting, though, is used by Paul both reluctantly and sarcastically . . . or at least facetiously. To boast is to speak of one's strength, not one's weaknesses. To boast is to glory in what others hold up as exemplary, not what the majority hold in contempt. But that is the irony of grace. Without Christ, I have nothing of which to boast; and with Christ, I boast I am nothing.

When Paul claimed that the power of Christ dwelt in him, "The compound verb here means to fix a tent or a habitation upon; and the figure is that of Christ abiding upon him as a tent spread over him during his temporary stay on earth." (Vincent, 356). Let that thought dwell in you.

My grace is sufficient for you. Could this simply and sublimely mean, "Paul, the fact that I have chosen you to serve me as an apostle, is more than you deserve. Let that suffice."

Compare that to what Paul said elsewhere:

> I thank Christ Jesus our Lord, who has strengthened me, because He considered me faithful, putting me into service, even though I was formerly a blasphemer and a persecutor and a violent aggressor, Yet I was shown mercy because I acted ignorantly in unbelief; and the grace of our Lord was more than abundant, with the faith and love which are found in Christ Jesus. It is a trustworthy statement, deserving full acceptance, that Christ Jesus came into the world to save sinners, among whom I am foremost of all. 1 Timothy 1.12–15

12.10: "Therefore I am well content with weaknesses, with insults, with distresses, with persecutions, with difficulties, for Christ's sake; for when I am weak, then I am strong."

After hearing Jesus say, "my grace is sufficient for you," Paul becomes content. He accepts the thorn in the flesh. Herein is an important lesson for us all: being content does not mean we like our circumstances. It does mean that we accept them and rely upon God, ultimately believing that His way is best. And that's what grace can do. It can keep us strong when we are weak. It can keep us focused on grace and not our problems. It is sufficient because it is from God.

Having gotten personal with Paul, let's get personal with ourselves. Let's talk about suffering, hurting, and pain. Let's talk about real life.

In Paul's life, we can see three everyday, real, "hey, this applies to me," situations.

> *The plea*: remove the problem—the problem of the thorn in the flesh. We all have problems we have asked God to remove. Pleading is a privilege.

> *The problem*: God says "no"—God's answer becomes another problem. Sometimes the bigger problem is not the original problem itself but accepting the original problem. Attitude is paramount when God says no.

> *The principle*: grace is enough—God's answer becomes the ultimate solution.

Paul's plea becomes our plea. How many tearful prayers have we cried? Paul's problem is our problem. How often have we wondered what or how much God wants from us? Will God's solution be shared? Like Paul, will we rise above suffering with grace?

It seems that people go to extremes when it comes to suffering. Some claim God is never connected to any suffering, while others blame Him for all suffering.

Biblically speaking, there are many reasons for suffering:

- Punishment for sin
- Consequences for sin
- Consequences of another's sin
- Temptations of Satan
- Testing by God
- Consequences of natural law
- Prevention by natural law
- Prevention of sin

In dealing with suffering, I have discovered that an important weapon is to examine our expectations. What were Paul's expectations of God? We know one of them: he wanted God to remove the thorn. Take a few moments and answer the following questions:

- What are my expectations of God?
- What are my expectations of God based on?
- What are my expectations of God for me?
- What should my expectations of God be?
- What should my expectations of God be based on?
- What should my expectations of God for me be?

Did you answer them? Now answer the following question: should we expect God to bless us better than He blessed His own Son? His Son was born in a stable, had no place to lay His head, was hunted, and finally betrayed, beaten, scourged, and crucified. Do we deserve to be treated better than that? Do the sinful deserve better than the Sinless?

What kind of life did the Giver of grace live? No wonder His grace is sufficient. He is sufficient. His grace came through His suffering. Disciples of Christ cannot expect to be treated better than God treated our Teacher. And yet, in reality, by grace, aren't we all treated better than Jesus? Think about what suffering we will not have to endure the next time we are suffering. Remember God's grace and think, "It is sufficient."

How would you answer the following question: life is filled with _____. How would Paul have answered it? The answer depends upon many circumstances.

- Present circumstances: what are we going through?
- Present actions: how are we handling it?
- Present state of mind: what are we thinking?
- Past experiences: have we experienced anything like this before?
- Personality: are we basically a pessimist or an optimist?
- People around us: do we have a good support base?
- Personal expectations: what are we expecting from life, from God, from ourselves, and others?
- Position in Christ: are we saved; are we growing more like Christ?

When we look at Paul's situation, we can see some of these answers. At the time he wrote 2 Corinthians, Paul's present circumstances were troubled. Read again the last part of chapter 11. I can honestly say that my life is very comfortable compared to Paul's. Paul handled his difficulties by praying, by waiting, and by surviving. Sometimes survival is all we can do today. Paul also confronted people, which caused some of his hurt. Being brave enough to face our tormentors takes grace, both for strength and for attitude. Paul's state of mind was hurt but hopeful. In the past, he himself had been a persecutor, so I think he was hurt more by the Corinthians mistreatment of him than by what unbelievers did to him. I will not even try to delve into Paul's personality, but

I don't think he was an optimist by birth; I do believe he was an optimist by rebirth. The apostle's support base was lousy, which intensified his relationship with Jesus. I think Paul's expectations were that Jesus would remove the thorn, but he also expected that God will be God, and that trumps all personal expectations. And finally, Paul's position in Christ as saved and as an apostle actually helped to create the thorn. But Paul knew Who sat on the throne. The one who sits on the throne of grace once wore thorns around His head, in His flesh, so Paul could receive grace.

Back to the question I asked at the beginning, "What first-century gift would you choose if you could have anything, or be anyone?" Paul's apostleship was a gift of grace. If I am correct concerning what Paul's thorn in the flesh is, then there is a wonderful lesson here that all of us can apply. We must do the work of God regardless of any side-effects or lack of pleasure and desire. Why? Because serving God is our gift of grace. And therefore, maybe, just maybe, our difficult predicament is God's grace itself. Let that discomforting thought sink in. Maybe what we are seeking to escape is, unknowingly, a place of grace. No wonder Jesus told Paul no. No wonder Jesus said, "My grace is sufficient." No wonder Paul silenced his cries for relief and release. Paul's life as an apostle grew increasingly grave, but it was also his place of grace (1 Cor. 15.9–10). What is ours? Whatever it is, God's grace is sufficient.

Questions

1. What were Paul's "qualifications" that he lists that gave him his qualifications as an apostle as opposed to the false apostles? 2 Cor. 11

2. What method of teaching did Paul employ in 2 Cor. 11?
_____ and _____

3. From the time the writing of 1 Corinthians 9.2 to the penning of 2 Corinthians, what had changed in the brethren's opinion of him? 2 Cor. 10-11

4. When faced with criticism regarding our walk as a Christian, what should we remember that is sufficient?

5. What should we remember when we get frustrated about not knowing?

6. Why was Paul given "a thorn in the flesh"?

_____

_____

7. In studying 2 Cor. 11 – 13, why do you think Paul boasts about his "weaknesses"? (clue – 11.30, 12.5,9, 13.4)

_____

_____

_____

_____

8. Why did God not take away Paul's "thorn in the flesh"? 2 Cor. 12.9

_____

_____

9. How is our common concept of a "thorn" different from the biblical definition of this word?

_____

_____

10. How could hardship, like Paul's "thorn in the flesh", be a blessing to us?

_____

_____

11. After asking three times for the "thorn in the flesh" to removed , Paul stopped asking and accepted Jesus' answer "My grace is sufficient for you". What can we learn and apply to our lives from this example? 2 Cor. 12.8-10

_____

_____

12. How is our modern definition of the word "sufficient" not adequate as compared to the biblical definition of this word as found in 2 Cor. 12.9?

_____

_____

_____

13. What lesson did God teach Paul concerning where strength is found? 2 Cor. 12.10

_____

_____

14. How does 2 Tim. 1.12-15 show an enlightenment that was gained by Paul once he accepted that Jesus' "grace was sufficient" (hint, 2 Cor. 12.10)?

_____

_____

_____

_____

15. How does Paul exemplify being content does not mean liking our circumstances?

_____

_____

_____

16. Consider our expectations of God. We should not expect God to bless us better than He blessed His own Son, should we? In what ways was Jesus' life difficult?

_____

_____

_____

_____

17. How could Jesus living through suffering make Him an example to us that "my grace is sufficient"?

_____

_____

18. Based on what we have learned about Jesus' grace being sufficient, how should this shape our thinking regarding doing the work of God?

_____

_____

3

The Grace That Is Understood

Colossians 1.15–20

How do you get someone's attention? Whisper behind their backs to someone else. But if you want to get someone thinking, what do you do then? Ask a question. If you want personal involvement in the process, make sure they know that the question is addressed directly to them. Jesus understood the power of asking questions, as did Socrates or any good teacher. My father said that during the first year of his law school, he was taught by using the Socratic method of teaching—that is by being asked questions. Apparently, for some, that method is very intimidating and humbling. By asking questions, we force people to become active in the process of learning. Asking questions is how the Supreme Court of the United States often examines the evidence. So, let's begin with some personal questions:

- How well do we truly understand God's grace?
- What does it mean to us to understand God's grace?
- If we are not growing and producing fruit, do we understand God's grace?

To me, these are not only thought-provoking questions, they are fear-producing and hope-inducing questions. Can we sincerely ask these questions and remain the same spiritually? Are asking these questions eternally life-changing? Are you ready to be changed? Understanding grace is the only way.

Let's look at the beginning texts:

Colossians1.3–6: We give thanks to God, the Father of our Lord Jesus Christ, praying always for you, since we heard of your faith in Christ Jesus and the love which you have for all the saints; because of the hope laid up for you in heaven, of which you previously heard in the word of truth, the gospel which has come to you, just as in all the world also it is constantly bearing fruit and increasing, even as it has been doing in you also since the day you heard of it and understood the grace of God in truth.

Colossians1.9–10: For this reason also, since the day we heard of it, we have not ceased to pray for you and to ask that you may be filled with the knowledge of His will in all spiritual wisdom and understanding, so that you will walk in a manner worthy of the Lord, to please Him in all respects, bearing fruit in every good work and increasing in the knowledge of God.

The purposes and goals of this chapter are as related as cause is to effect. As what goes up must come down; what is changed by grace must grow and produce fruit.

Our first goal is to better understand grace by filling ourselves with Jesus and the knowledge of His will, which is the theme of Colossians. This takes knowledge, which must not only be studied but accepted and applied personally. Filling ourselves with the knowledge of Jesus Christ naturally, or should I say spiritually, leads to the second goal: walking in a manner worthy of and pleasing to Jesus by growing and producing fruit. One leads to the other; one must lead to the other. Can we see all that happening in our lives?

In examining our purposes and goals, our thought process is very simple: the better we know, understand, and accept a truth, the more it affects us and changes us—if we apply it. To illustrate, do you remember learning how to drive and your father trying to warn you about the "blind spot?" I do. He did. I didn't. No, I foolishly thought to myself, "Blindspot? I don't see a blind spot? (ironic, no?). Maybe my dad has a blind spot, but I don't have a . . ."

Please interrupt this self-absorbed thought and replace it by the blaring sound of a honking horn, a near-crash, and a quick decision on my part not to change lanes . . . because out of nowhere—or more accurately, out of my blind spot—a car appeared . . . and it also appeared my dad was right . . . and I wasn't as right as I could have been. (OK, I was wrong!)

Another example is the food we eat. The better we understand the facts of good eating habits, the less likely we are to stuff our face with the stuff that is stuffing our waistlines, bellies, and thighs.

Read what follows slowly: can you understand that you need to understand what I mean when I say "understand"? Did you understand that question? Let me explain. When I use the word "understood" as in "the grace that is understood," I am not referring to a regurgitation of mere facts—I am speaking of the effect these facts have in our lives. I am talking about our relationship to these facts and to the "Factor." I am referring to how these facts change us for all of eternity on this side of eternity.

Notice the definitions of the word understood (*epiginōsko*) which is found in Colossians 1.6:

1. "sometimes implies a special participation in the object known....lays stress on participation in the truth." (Vine, 639).
   Notice in this definition the personal action involved.

2. "to become thoroughly acquainted with, to know thoroughly; to know accurately, know well...." (Thayer, 237). Notice in this definition the completeness of the knowledge.

Biblical "understanding" is not about our feelings concerning what we know; it is not about our intellectual grasp either. It is about how what we know affects us every day. It is about how what we know changes us from day to day. It is about how what we know determines our eternal destination because of its effects and changes in our lives this side of eternity. That's a powerful understanding! The Amplified Bible expands our understanding by combining both meanings of *epiginōsko*:

Colossians1.6 (Amplified): Which has come to you. Indeed, in the whole world [that Gospel] is bearing fruit and still is growing [by its own inherent power], even as it has done among yourselves ever since the day you first heard and came to know and understand the grace of God in truth. [You came to know the grace or undeserved favor of God in reality, deeply and clearly and thoroughly, becoming accurately and intimately acquainted with it.]

How does what we believe about Jesus change and affect our behavior every day? The understanding goes far deeper than what He did for us on Calvary. It begins with Who Jesus is—Who He is in reference to both His Father and us. Knowing who Jesus is gives Calvary its empowering message. Understanding Jesus is understanding grace.

Have you ever pondered how your life would be different if you were not a believer? Hesitatingly, I ask, would it be different?

A poll surveyed a hundred members from various types of churches about the significance of the cross. This is the question asked: "Would it make any difference in your life if Christ had not died on the cross?" Here are the results (Earles, 97):

45% said they didn't think it would make any difference.
25% said they thought so, but when asked what the difference would be, they weren't sure.
20% said it would make all the difference in how they lived and believed.
10% said they didn't know, because they didn't understand what the cross was all about.

Is there something wrong with this picture? Only 20 percent knew the cross made a difference in how they lived and in what they believed? How sad. The cross is at the very center of Christian faith because the cross is a gift of grace. But within the context of this chapter, it is not just the healing effects of the cross for me that I am concerned with, but even more, Who died for me. How can we say we understand Jesus if we don't understand the cross? How can we say we understand the cross if we don't understand Jesus? How can we understand the effects of the cross on us, if we don't understand the effects of the cross on Jesus?

Let's understand Jesus . . . so that we can understand grace . . . so that we can be changed . . . so that we can grow and produce fruit. That's the purpose and result of understanding grace.

According to Colossians, Jesus Christ is—and this is the beginning of understanding—the fullness of God . . . the cause of holiness . . . the foundation of us walking in a manner worthy of Himself . . . the One whom we must understand in order to understand grace. Jesus is the cause and effect. Let's rephrase our purpose. If we understand Jesus and are filled up with Christ, then we will live like Him. That's understanding grace. That's why Paul begins by exalting and examining Jesus. So let's read our text, Col.1.15–20:

> [15] He is the image of the invisible God, the firstborn of all creation.
>
> [16] For by Him all things were created, both in the heavens and on earth, visible and invisible, whether thrones or dominions or rulers or authorities—all things have been created through Him and for Him.
>
> [17] He is before all things, and in Him all things hold together.
>
> [18] He is also head of the body, the church; and He is the beginning, the firstborn from the dead, so that He Himself will come to have first place in everything.
>
> [19] For it was the Father's good pleasure for all the fullness to dwell in Him,
>
> [20] and through Him to reconcile all things to Himself, having made peace through the blood of His cross; through Him, I say, whether things on earth or things in heaven.

Charles Spurgeon said something I will never forget,

> There is something exceedingly improving to the mind in a contemplation of the Divinity. It is a subject so vast, that all our thoughts are lost in its immensity; so deep, that our pride is drowned in its infinity. Other subjects we can compass and grapple with; in them we feel a kind of self-content, and go our way with the thought, "Behold I am wise." But when we come to this master-science, finding that our plumb-line cannot sound its depth, and that our eagle eye cannot see its height, we turn away with the thought that vain man would be wise, but he is like a wild ass's colt; and with solemn exclamation, "I am but of yesterday, and know

nothing." No subject of contemplation will tend more to humble the mind, than thoughts of God. (Spurgeon (in Packer, 13–14))

Are we ready to improve our minds, our souls, and our walk with Christ by studying God in the flesh, by understanding grace, by contemplating the grace-giver?

This ancient hymn, which is what many scholars believe the text contains, can be divided into two sections or verses:

1. Jesus is the fullness of God in physical creation
2. Jesus is the fullness of God in spiritual creation

The first refers to the original creation, which is recorded in Genesis; the second refers to the new creation—those who understand grace.

As we organize the material, we will further divide the text into two sections, one theological and the other practical. Such an order makes sense because of what Paul said in Colossians 1.9–10:

Theological—that you may be filled with the knowledge of His will in all spiritual wisdom and understanding.

Practical—so that you will walk in a manner worthy of the Lord.

Below we will distinguish these by the phrases filled with knowledge (theological) and walking worthily (practical). Think of the first as a noun and the second as a verb. Think of the first as the cause and the second as the effect.

Very quickly, let me make an important historical and yet applicable point. Two extremes of "Christianity" have divorced these two principles, the theological and the practical.

The first extreme is a "Christianity" that is all knowledge but without experiencing that knowledge. That is an "ivory-tower-Christianity." That would never happen, right? Sadly, too many times it does. People claiming to understand grace have locked themselves away from the world, whether behind mortar or pretend walls. How can they walk if they are, for all practical concerns, imprisoned? History is filled with "academic Christianity." A less-institutionalized example would be a local church that is filled with the right doctrines and yet also filled with so much trouble. How can that be? How can they be filled with the right doctrines of Christ, but not be filled with Christ? They have knowledge, but ironically they do not have understanding. And without understanding, they are not producing fruit. A Christianity where knowledge reigns without personal change does not understand grace.

Extremes beget extremes. So, possibly out of reaction, we have witnessed the exact opposite where a sham and shallow "Christianity" disdains knowledge; where Christianity is no longer about the Man and His plan but has deteriorated into a simplified "better-felt-than-told-Christianity." This isn't a life-changing experience; it is just feelings replacing repentance. Instead of true change, these interpersonal, unexplainable experiences, and feelings have displaced revealed knowledge about the person of Christ. External, objective truth does not exist to these "religious hippies." The central figure of this counterfeit Christianity is not Christ, but "me." If truth is not causing the experience, can it be a true experience? Think about that!

So, what does the Holy Spirit through Paul reveal about the grace-giver that I need to understand? Let's begin in 1.15–17, where Christ is the fullness of God in physical creation.

Understand Jesus is Fully Divine

Colossians 1:15a: He is the image of the invisible God.

<u>Filled With Knowledge</u>

Like a prism showing the invisible colors of light, Jesus makes the invisible seen. "He who has seen Me has seen the Father," Jesus said to Thomas (Jn.14.9).

Consider the following:

> To call Christ the image of God is to say that in Him the being and nature of God have been perfectly manifested—that in Him the invisible has become visible. (Bruce)

When we consider Jesus as the *eikon*, or in English, the "icon" of God, maybe this explains the reluctance of some of the modern Jews to accept Jesus as the Son of God. (2nd Commandment). I can only wonder. However, Jesus is not a graven image, but the real image!

Other scriptures teach the same theological lesson about Jesus—same lesson, different language:

- John1.1–3: "In the beginning was the Word, and the Word was with God, and the Word was God. He was in the beginning with God. All things came into being through Him, and apart from Him nothing came into being that has come into being."
- Hebrews1.3: "And He is the radiance of His glory and the exact representation of His nature, and upholds all things by the word of His power. When He had made purification of sins, He sat down at the right hand of the Majesty on high."
- 2 Corinthians 4.4: "In whose case the god of this world has blinded the minds of the unbelieving so that they might not see the light of the gospel of the glory of Christ, who is the image of God."
- Philippians 2.5–6: "Have this attitude in yourselves which was also in Christ Jesus, who, although He existed in the form of God, did not regard equality with God a thing to be grasped."
- John14.8–9: "Philip said to Him, "Lord, show us the Father, and it is enough for us." Jesus said to him, "Have I been so long with you, and yet you have not come to know Me, Philip? He who has seen Me has seen the Father; how can you say, 'Show us the Father'?"

Our grace-giver is the image of the invisible God.

Walking Worthily

How can you see the invisible? The answer is simple—one can only see the invisible when the unseen becomes seen. So, can we know God even though He is invisible? Can we ever have a relationship with this invisible God? Yes, we can know the invisible God through the visible Christ. This is where Jesus' incarnation is essential in understanding the Father and Spirit, who did not incarnate. Through Jesus, who lived pure in the flesh, we learn about the Father, who is pure spirit. Jesus is an image in the sense that people can directly experience God through Him.

How can we today have that same experience? We did not witness Jesus' walk in the flesh. We did not see "visible Deity." Yet, there is a way. We can experience God by getting to know Jesus. Truly knowing Jesus involves truly understanding Jesus. The result is that the knowledge changes both our invisible and visible selves. We can help others experience God by helping them get to know Jesus—by teaching Jesus and living Jesus—by walking worthy of the Lord. We experience Jesus by walking like Jesus.

Now what I am about to say is exciting. The same word, image/*eikon*, which describes Jesus, is used of us in a more limited sense. That fact should be enlightening, exciting, and exacting.

Colossians 3.10: And have put on the new self [lit., man] who is being renewed [lit., renovated] to a true knowledge, according to the image [*eikon*] of the One who created him.

What is our goal? To look like Jesus! Why? Because Jesus made the invisible God, visible. And our goal is the same. Are we up to our goal? When we are holy, spiritual, loving, and truthful, we are living like Jesus lived. We are living grace. When we mirror Jesus, we are experiencing the image of God within ourselves. In a far more limited sense, by our lives, we can also make visible the invisible God. Making visible the invisible within our lives is understanding grace. Wow! What an awesome thought. Walk worthy!

Understand Jesus is Fully Human

Colossians 1.15b: The first-born of all creation.

<u>Filled With Knowledge</u>

Just as assuredly that Jesus is fully God, He is fully Man. In our culture, "first-born" does not carry the significance it once did. For us, about the only guarantee that the firstborn has is that he doesn't get hand-me-downs . . . unless he has an older cousin . . . or until . . . his younger brother grows taller!

In Jewish eyes, being first-born resulted in a privileged position.

"In the rabbis the term denotes the special position of Israel, the law, Adam, or the Messiah, with a reference either to the special love of God or to the special qualities of those to whom the term applies.." (Kittel, 967)

Jesus is not just a first-born, nor the first-born. He is the First-born of all creation. This text has caused arguments from the time of Arius to Jehovah's Witnesses today. Was Jesus just a created being? If so, then the rest of Colossians is just a waste of papyri (2.9).

The term first-born can refer to rank, not just time. Have you ever noticed the repeating theme in Genesis, where the first to be born is not accepted as the first-born?

- Cain versus Abel
- Cain versus Seth
- Ishmael versus Isaac
- Esau versus Jacob
- Leah versus Rachel
- Reuben versus Judah (4th born; Gen. 49)
- Ten sons of Jacob versus Joseph
- Manasseh versus Ephraim (Gen. 48)

Let's discuss this concept of "first-born." I like reading biblical genealogies—they make for quick reading! The eyes just skim over the names that the tongue would stumble over, so why slow down? The mind prepares itself for some numbing reading, eyes glaze over, brain disengaged....

Then bam! The brain kicks in because the eyes saw something other than just a bunch of unpronounceable syllables. Words. Real words. Words that actually form a coherent sentence. Wow! Time to pay attention again! Biblical genealogies reveal surprises that appear out of nowhere. Mysteries can be solved. Lessons can be learned. Surprises can, well, surprise.

For example, Joseph is not in the lineage of Jesus. Did you ever wonder why God chose to record the story of Joseph, which makes up 13 out of the last 14 chapters of Genesis? Isn't the Old Testament supposed to point to Jesus?

Yes, there are many lessons from Joseph's life of forgiveness and fortitude. And there are the deeper type/antitype layers foreshadowing Christ. And yet in one of the many genealogies, we learn another reason why:

> 1 Chronicles 5.1–2: Now the sons of Reuben the firstborn of Israel (for he was the firstborn, but because he defiled his father's bed, his birthright was given to the sons of Joseph the son of Israel; so that he is not enrolled in the genealogy according to the birthright. Though Judah prevailed over his brothers, and from him came the leader, yet the birthright belonged to Joseph).

The story of Joseph is the story of the first-born who was not born first. The first-born, according to patriarchal customs, was the cultural double winner—blessings and birthright. The first-born received a double portion of his father's inheritance, which might explain why two lots in the Promise Land were given to Joseph in his sons Manasseh and Ephraim. Contrary to birth order and even paternity, through Joseph, his sons become the first-born of Jacob. And then on top of that, Manasseh, who was born first, is replaced by Ephraim as the first-born (Gen. 48.13–20).

In Genesis, the first-born often disappoints. Sometimes the first-born is replaced due to no disgrace of his own (Rom. 9). Is this a lesson of humility? Of man's ways not being God's? Of appearance and reality not being equal? Are we to learn something about grace? Oh, there are probably tons of lessons.

Messianic prophecy declares, "I also shall make him My first-born, the highest of the kings of earth" (Ps. 89.27). Being first-born is a position of rank, not a position of birth. Jesus was made, not born, first-born because obviously He was not "born" first.

When we get to the New Testament, we see the emphasis on Jesus Christ being the first-born (Col. 1) and even Jesus' spiritual descendants being called the first-born (Heb. 12.23, lit., first-born ones). I wonder . . . did Jesus and His followers take the place of another first-born? Did another first-born puff himself up with pride? Did another first-born disgrace himself? Find the answer, and you get another surprise. "Then you shall say to Pharaoh, 'Thus says the LORD, Israel is My son, My firstborn'" (Ex. 4.22). Jesus became the new first-born. Jesus became the new Israel.

Over and over again, the first to be born is not the first-born. Jesus assuredly was not the first to be born in the flesh, but He is the first-born. Jesus is undoubtedly, according to this text and the New Testament, first-born and head over all creation.

And yet the expression "first-born of all creation" does not necessitate an understanding of Jesus as created:

> Even the Jews referred to God as the "first-born of the world." (Brumback, 118)

And yet again, for the sake of argument, let's surmise that for Jesus to be first-born of all creation, Jesus Himself must also be created. Should we deny Jesus was created? Yes . . . and no! I love answers like that. In spirit, yes, we should deny any origin for Jesus. In body, no, for how can we deny the creation of His body? Jesus' spirit is without beginning; Jesus' body is not. To help us understand the connection between Jesus as first-born of all creation and Jesus being part of creation, let's make some comparisons:

> If Jesus is the first-born among brethren (Rom. 8.29), then Jesus must be a brother.

> If Jesus is the first-born from the dead (Col. 1.18), then Jesus must have been dead and then resurrected.

> What does being a brother to humans and dying as a human entail? Being human.

> Are humans created? Yes. Was Jesus human? Yes, in body. In that, and only in that, Jesus, our grace-giver was and is created (Heb. 10.5). Only in body, not in spirit.

Colossians 1.15 shows Jesus' relationship to God (i.e., the image of the invisible God) and His relationship to us (i.e., the first-born of all creation). The divine being is not created. The human being is.

Within the context of the Colossian heresy (i.e., Eastern Gnosticism mangled with Jewish tradition), connecting Jesus to the flesh is paramount to destroying the false philosophy of Gnosticism. Therefore I do not see the benefit of simply having the term "first-born of all creation" to only mean "the One who has priority to and sovereignty over all creation," a phrase borrowed from Wuest. Even more so, I see denying such a connection as destructive to the core of Christianity.

Why is Jesus over all creation? He created it. Why is He the first-born? He took on flesh and is preeminent among us. Further proof of this interpretation is found by asking, "When does the term 'firstborn' again appear?" The answer is in reference again to His fleshly experience—Jesus is the first-born from the dead.

See, there is nothing controversial about that at all. True knowledge destroys false conclusions. And true knowledge leads to that knowledge having a profound impact upon my grace-filled life.

Walking Worthily

Jesus being the first-born, shows His preeminence. I am not sure we should use the term "second-born" to describe us, but we are brothers and sisters to the first-born (Heb. 2.11–12). Since we are part of creation, is Jesus preeminent in our lives? Are we functioning as creation was designed by God to operate? Are we trying to live in the flesh as Jesus lived in His flesh?

Our Grace-Giver is first-born of all creation (Col. 1.15b). Does that include us? Walk worthy!

Understand Jesus Is Fully Creator

Colossians 1.16: "For by Him all things were created, both in the heavens and on earth, visible and invisible, whether thrones or dominions or rulers or authorities all things have been created through Him and for Him. Moffat's translation reads: all comes from Him, all lives by Him, all ends in Him."

Filled with Knowledge

This verse helps explain Jesus being the first-born (preeminent) of all creation. Take the first word of v. 16 (i.e., "for") and understand it to mean "because." Not only is Jesus first-born among us because He is greater than us, Jesus is the first-born among us because He created us.

Surely, modern-day Christians do not deny this knowledge, do they? Sadly many do but in disguise. They teach a "theistic evolution." In other words, Christ was not the Creator of all things, but rather Creator of all things that evolved into all things. Is this nothing more than semantics? No. To compare creation to evolution would be like comparing a painted work of art to a can of paint or the paint accidentally splattered on the floor. Is Jesus the Creator or the Evolver? Is creation a masterpiece or a drop cloth? Filling ourselves with the wonder of creation fills us with wonder of the Creator.

Walking Worthily

A good question to ask is, "What is the effect on our lives if we believe Jesus is the Evolver of all things?" In other words, how does that affect our walk? Without wanting to be guilty of over-generalizing, does the need and desire to concede within one area lead to conceding in others? How strong are those who are willing to believe in theistic evolution willing to alter another "creation" – the resurrection of Christ? Is that real or just a metaphor? Doesn't the example of Jesus' power in creating life out of nothing give credence to the power to bring life back to something?

Let's make some "since" of Jesus being the Creator:

Since Christ created all things, we owe our allegiance and our worship to Him. He created us and recreates us.

Since Christ created all things, He understands us and our needs better than we do. He fulfills us.

Since Christ created all things, nothing can hurt us if we rest in Him. No power in the world is superior to His. He protects us.

Since Christ created all things, I am special.

Since Christ created all things, and since I understand this, my life of grace is eternally changed. He is my guide.

Understand Jesus is Fully Sovereign

Colossians 1.17: "He is before all things, and in Him all things hold together."

<u>Filled with Knowledge</u>

J. B. Phillips' paraphrase:

"[Jesus] is both the first principle and the holding principle of the whole scheme of creation. Jesus is not only before all things; we are also told in Him all things hold together. He is the glue."

The philosopher may seek for a principle of coherence, a unity amid all the diversity of the world of sense; but in the Son the believer finds the true principle of coherence. It is His power alone which holds the Creation together. (Colcar, source unknown)

Obviously, deism is a false theology. (Deism is a religious and philosophical belief which asserts that Deity created the universe and then stepped away, never interacting with His creation through miracles, inspiration, or even answering prayers.) Jesus is involved in everyday life. He is not the Evolver, but He is the "Involver."

<u>Walking Worthily</u>

Jesus did not create the world and then walk away. His leadership and Lordship over creation are essential for every moment of every day. Were He to take His hands off us for a minute, we would fall apart. So many people wonder, when life is hard, "Where is God; Where is Jesus?" The answer is, if Jesus is not near, life itself ceases to be. Without Jesus, there is no good and no absence of good. All that remains is nothing. And if there were something, it would be chaos beyond the brokenness that any of us have endured.

Jesus is the one who keeps existence going. He makes the sun to shine, the rain to fall, the earth to rotate, the seasons to come and go. He is the one who continues to grant life to our bodies. But doesn't natural law govern these things? Yes. But Who created that law? At any given moment, He could withdraw His hand, and we would be finished. The implications are simple:

> We ought to be humble. We are not independent in the fullest sense of the word. Without Him, we could do nothing. Even the nonbeliever owes his very life to the mercy of the Savior.

> We ought to be grateful. Every day we live is a gift of grace from our Lord.

Jesus sustains us. My maternal grandmother was like that. When "Grandmommy" was alive, all the uncles, aunts, cousins, and so on would get together. Family reunions were held every year. A couple of years after her death, it all ended for our side of the family. Today, since my mom also has passed, my dad sustains our family. Do you have a relative like that?

If Jesus holds all things together, and if He is holding my family and me, then my family will be held together. The sufficiency of Christ is not only in terms of our salvation but also in every area of our lives.

- I understand Jesus can fill the emptiness of loneliness as He filled the emptiness of space.
- I understand Jesus is stronger than my trials because He overcame His trials.
- I understand Jesus' word created physical life and recreates spiritual life.
- I understand Jesus' gifts of grace are all I need today and every day.
- I understand that without Jesus, I fall apart.

We are now ready to proceed to the second division of Paul's great glorification of Christ. The Holy Spirit turns from Jesus the Creator of the first creation to Jesus the Creator of the second creation or re-creation. Re-creation, recreating, is a common theme throughout the Bible. For example, the flood story should not be viewed simply as a destruction of the old, but as a new creation from the old. Notice the similarities between the two creation stories in Genesis (Brueggemann, pp.73ff):

Old Earth	New Earth
Earth covered with water, 1.2-6	Earth covered with water, 7.17-20
Command to multiply, 1.28	Command to multiply, 9.1,7
Man in God's image, 1.26–27	Man in God's image, 9.6
Permission to eat 1.29, 2.16	Permission to eat, 9.3
Prohibition on eating, 2.17	Prohibition on eating, 9.4
Man over animals, 1.28	Man over animals, 9.2
God rested, 2.2–3	God rested, 8.21, 9.15

Recreation from old to new, from curse to blessing, from death to life, is a recurring Biblical theme.

- From barrenness to blessings of children. Sarah, Rebekah, Rachel, and more.

- From a valley of dry bones to an exceedingly great army (Ezek. 37). This has to be one of the most imaginative and picturesque stories of grace.

- From a cross, to a tomb, to a rolled away stone, to an empty grave, to a resurrected Christ. And then Jesus takes His resurrected body, a body rescued from the old creation, and ascends with it into the sky where no doubt another transformation takes place in the twinkling of an eye (1 Cor. 15.52).

Over and over in the Old Testament, Deity takes physical creation, along with its curses, and re-creates blessings. This foreshadows a greater new beginning in the New Covenant, the covenant of grace. Over and over, the story of physical re-creation forecasts a greater re-creation. He who is central to the beginning of everything physical is now lauded as central to the beginning of everything spiritual. From creation to re-creation, from the beginning, continuing, and bettering of everything, we find Jesus. Because of the first creation's connection to Jesus, creation functions as designed. Its only failures are curses from man's sin (Rom. 8.19–22). Because of the second creation's connection to Jesus, we are to function as designed. And again, our only failures arise from sin.

As Ralph Martin said,

> As early as 1913 the German scholar, E. Norden, had arranged these verses into a hymnic form and detected certain liturgical traits....It is apparent from this division that the stanzas cover two subjects: Christ and creation (verses 15-18a) and Christ and the Church (verses 18b-20). Moreover, the two parts are comparable in a number of ways and certain stylistic peculiarities are present which cannot be there by chance. For example, we may note the repetition of words and phrases in the two halves, and in some cases the words are repeated in exactly the same position in each stanza. A. M. Hunter has observed that three pairs of lines are precisely correspondent in the two parts of the hymn. The vocabulary also is unusual and the whole 'betrays the hand of an exacting composer' who penned this noble tribute to exhibit the primacy of Christ in the twin realms of Creation and Redemption. (Martin, 50-51)

Understand Jesus Is Fully Lord

Colossians 1.18: "He is also head of the body, the church."

<u>Filled With Knowledge</u>

To be the head is to be in charge, which is to be obeyed. And yet, sadly, have you ever heard someone try to separate Jesus being Savior from His being Lord? They are combating what has been called "Lordship Salvation." Their purpose is to supposedly teach salvation by grace. And yet, they actually end up denying the need for grace. Why would I need grace unless I sin even after being saved? To them, accepting Jesus as Lord upon our salvation implies obedience, and obedience implies salvation by works. Therefore they have to deny Jesus is both our Lord and Savior! Amazing. Sadly amazing. Accepting God's grace does not deny obedience. Faith is always obedient (Heb. 11; Rom. 6) because faith is trusting God. The faithful understand God's grace means they understand they don't deserve God's grace, nor do they deserve to even obey God. How's that for not believing in salvation by works? I do not believe

I even have the right to obey God because I have sinned. To serve my Lord is to be His image on earth. Who deserves that? To teach that we can accept Jesus as Savior without Him also being Lord of our life is "headless horseman theology." You can't have a body without a head; physical life requires it, as does spiritual life.

There are many metaphors for the church, but I wonder if any of them have any more significance than Jesus as the head and the church as His body:

> So far as the organic relationship is concerned, Christ and His people are viewed together as a living entity: Christ the head, supplying life and exercising control and direction; His people are His body, individually His limbs and organs, under His control, obeying His direction, performing His work. (Colbruce, source unknown)

If I am not required to make Jesus my Lord, then His body is not required to have a head.

> Col.2.10: And in Him you have been made complete, and He is the head over all rule and authority.

> Col.2.19: And not holding fast to the head, from whom the entire body, being supplied and held together by the joints and ligaments, grows with a growth which is from God.

Think . . . what is the purpose of a head? Isn't it to communicate commands to the body? Who is in charge, the head or the body? Are we listening? Are we even connected?

Walking Worthily

This should go without saying, but it must be said. The church is not my church, nor your church . . . it is Christ's church (Matt.16.18). He founded it; He is in charge of it; He is the head. Yes, I understand there is a form in which it is ours in the sense of participation, just as Paul could call Christ's gospel, "my gospel" (Rom. 2.16). But I am not talking about that. I am talking about ownership. I am talking about leadership. I am talking about Lordship. It is Christ's!

Humor sometimes has a sharp tongue. Many jokes begin with, "Did you hear the one about . . ." Well, this joke is no joke, whether the story is actually true or not. The overall situation is too sad, too common, and too true to be funny:

Did you hear the one about the man who drove into a small town looking for the church of Christ? The stranger asked a man he found whittling on the courthouse steps. "Church of Christ, you want?" asked the whittler. "Well now, there's a big church over there sometimes called the Baptist Church, but it really belongs to Mr. Jones. He runs it. There is a beautiful church on yonder corner some call Presbyterian, but it belongs to Mr. McGregor. He runs it. There's a building around the corner I've heard called a synagogue, but Mr. Stein calls the shots there. Then there's the cathedral, but Mr. O'Murphy is the boss there. You know, stranger, I don't believe Christ has a church in this town.

Regardless of the name on the sign, sometimes the name (i.e., preacher, pastor) under the church name is the real boss. Sometimes it is the name not even on the sign that is the obvious head. There is no "power behind the throne" in Christ's church.

In this day, when more and more emphasis is on making the church like a corporation with a single human as CEO, it is important that we remember that the church is not a corporation. We are His body. We are to do His bidding. He is the one who is calling the shots. Do we know what this means?

The church is most effective when we trust His ways rather than our own.

The healthy church spends much time in prayer seeking God's direction.

We must remember that no individual can change a human life . . . only God can. Our job is not to call people to an organization, but to Christ.

In Paul's great illustration of the "members" of the body in 1 Corinthians 12, he purposely did not call any member the head. That position has already been filled. To understand grace means I grow from the head.

To paraphrase our Head, the kingdom of God can be compared to a man who suffers from rebellious body parts. He who has ears to hear, let him hear the parable of the rebellious body:

> I never should have gone to the party, not feeling like I did. If I'd stayed at home, those headlines might never have appeared. I'd been wanting to get a new pair of glasses, needed to get some. I saw some that complimented my face, but I couldn't get them and that new pair of shoes I'd been wanting, too. I got shoes.
>
> I noticed trouble brewing as I got dressed. My eyes started blurring on me. I should have gotten worried about that, but I was sidetracked when my left arm informed me it wasn't going to the party. Said he was staying home to nurse a mild ache he's had for a couple of weeks. I argued that he'd worked with the rest of my body with that same ailment for a while now, why should that stop him tonight? He said he just wasn't going. Of course, that meant I also lost the use of my left hand, as it had to go with the arm. Hand didn't want to be "left out" either, but what can I do? I'll miss those guys, I thought, as I left them behind. It would be hard to balance a plate and eat from it with just one hand, too.
>
> My vision worried me, once I got outside. It would blur, then focus, then blur again. I even suffered total blindness a few times that night. I guess my eyes were telling me they were upset by my decision to shoe the feet instead of getting new glasses. They never would talk to me about it, but I assume that was the problem. Those eyes of mine never have been good at talking things out. Guess I should be thankful they are eyes and not my mouth.
>
> Most of my body was glad to be at the party. Hand enjoyed clasping fellow hands in greetings. Feet were proud to move about the room, showing off the new shoes. Stomach was hungry, and ears enjoyed the sounds of laughter, conversation, and music. In one of their clearer moments, eyes spotted a tempting dish on the table. Looked delicious. I'd never seen a dish like that. Nose took a whiff and declared it worth tasting. But when the spoon reached my mouth, teeth refused to open. They wouldn't budge. I told them I was hungry, stomach was growling, eyes and nose chimed in, begging teeth just to try it. No way. Teeth said it didn't matter if the whole body was for eating it; it had to get past them first. They'd never had that food and weren't about to have it now. Even when I forced a bit past the clenched jaws, they barely chewed it, then declared they were spitting it out in five seconds, so I ran for a napkin. I had to give in. Teeth never gave that food a chance.
>
> It was then I noticed I wasn't hearing anything. Ears were on strike. Said

nobody ever paid them any attention, so they were shutting down till they got some respect. I told them a lot of my body parts are like them—valuable, not always appreciated—but they weren't listening to me, either. I was really having a hard time functioning now, trying to read lips through blurred eyes, unable to hear a thing. Stomach was steadily increasing volume in growling for food, but teeth insisted we only eat the same old stuff we could get every day at home.

Suddenly, a pain ripped through my side. My intestines informed me that it was just a sample of what they were capable of inflicting. I asked what they wanted and was told I had hurt them by feeding on some raw peanuts. I assured them I'd eaten nothing that night, but they said this was a week ago. I'd hurt them, and they wanted me to know it. They'd tried sulking about it, but when nobody noticed, they decided to make waves and get revenge. Boy, did they.

I left the party, stumbling, bent over at the waist, not hearing the goodbyes of my hosts, hungry, angry at the parts of my body, which made the evening a disaster. I went home, determined to see a doctor soon. I can't go on living like this. Parablius, 9

If we don't listen to the head, we don't function according to His purpose, and we don't function according to the needs of the body either. Not listening hurts us because it hurts more than just us. Not listening hurts us because it hurts the body . . . which is us.

Listen to the head. After all, doesn't Jesus know best? Grace knows the answer. Walk worthy!

Understand Jesus Is Fully Able to Resurrect Us

Colossians 1.18: "He is the beginning, the first-born from the dead."

<u>Filled with Knowledge</u>

Jesus being the first-born from the dead, declares His resurrection and implies mine. Christ is the first-fruits (1 Cor. 15.23). This does not mean no one was raised from the dead previously (e.g., Lazarus), but rather no one was raised from the dead to never die again. When reading the following section, you will notice that I flit back and forth between Christ's resurrection and ours. Biblically speaking, they cannot be separated. Grace speaks to both.

Satan combated the resurrection doctrine in the first-century and continues today. Satan's schemes should be a clue to us that the resurrection is an essential doctrine by witnessing the efforts of Satan to denounce, deny, and discredit it. If it is important enough for Satan to pay attention to it, then it is important enough for us Christians to pay attention to it.

In 1 Corinthians 15, Paul had to fight against deniers of this great fact. Paul connected Christ's resurrection to ours and took both resurrections very seriously and personally. In 15.12–19, we have his inspired denial of the resurrection's denial:

- **IF** Christ is preached resurrected, **THEN** we will be resurrected v.12
- **IF** we are not resurrected, **THEN** not even Christ was resurrected v.13
- IF Christ has not been raised, **THEN** our preaching is in vain v.14
- IF Christ has not been raised, **THEN** we are false witnesses against God v.15
- IF Christ has not been raised, **THEN** your faith is worthless v.17
- IF Christ has not been raised, **THEN** you are still in your sins v.17
- IF Christ has not been raised, **THEN** those who have fallen asleep have perished v.18
- **IF** we have hoped in Christ in this life only, **THEN** we are of all men most to be pitied v.19

Today, Satan does not need to fight too hard against the resurrection doctrine. Today, the resurrection of the dead is a sadly neglected subject. In the first-century, it was not neglected. Satan needed to cause hearers to sneer at the resurrection of Christ (Acts 17.32). Why is it neglected today?

First, maybe we don't truly understand grace like they did in the first-century. However, that is somewhat judgmental, even if true. So let me suggest some other possibilities that might not hit as close to home. After all, we don't want to take the subject of grace personally, do we?

Second, we have to admit that, unfortunately, there is a faction among many intellectual elite—claiming allegiance to Christianity—that actually denies the bodily resurrection of Christ. And if Christ is not physically resurrected, then it becomes a nonevent for us. Of course, Satan also combated a belief in the resurrection in the first-century by denying Jesus came in the flesh—Gnosticism. Same result; different tactics. And if getting people to deny our resurrection as a reality (1 Cor. 15.12) does not work, then Satan will get people to deny it on another level—namely, the resurrection is already past (2 Tim. 2.18). Either way, Satan spent a lot of time in the first-century combating the resurrection of both Christ and of people.

Third, it is neglected because we choose not to emphasize it. The writer of Hebrews considers the resurrection of the dead to be first principles (Heb. 6.1-2). Do we? The faithful refused to deny their faith and were tortured, not accepting their release, so that they might obtain a better resurrection (Heb. 11.35). Would we? Do you think they understood grace?

Fourth, do we focus so much on heaven as our eternal destination that we forget about the resurrection of our bodies? Do we realize that we are not designed by God to exist without a body? Read 2 Corinthians 5 and realize that our spirits are designed to have a body, both here and now and in the resurrection. Without the body, the spirit is "uncomfortable."

Obviously, Satan does not want us to believe in either Jesus' resurrection or ours. Why is the resurrection such a cornerstone doctrine? Could we be missing something still? Is there something intricately tied with the resurrection that either has not been revealed or else has been, but we have missed it somehow.

Let's test our knowledge. According to the Bible, why is there a need for a resurrection? Go ahead and think about this before reading on. Why is there a resurrection?

Do we need a body to go to heaven? Apparently not—Paul desired to die and go to heaven (Phil. 1.21-23). Do we need a body to have our personal identity? Again, apparently not—Jesus saw both Moses and Elijah on the mountain, and the resurrection had not yet come (Matt. 17.3).

So, if I do not need a body to go to heaven, and if I do not need a body to be me, what is the purpose of resurrection? Let me ask some more questions that will lead us to the answer.

- When did Christ defeat Satan?
- When will I ultimately defeat Satan?

Yes, I know we defeat Satan here and now, but there is a sense in which Satan still wins because I will die. Jesus died. The last enemy that will be abolished is death (1 Cor. 15.26). If there is no resurrection, Satan wins. The purpose and need of the resurrection are for God to defeat Satan—and for us to be given another gift of grace.

Maybe if we understood grace better, we would understand how this great doctrine of Christ being the first-born from the dead, never to die again, affects our walking worthily. So keep reading . . .

<u>Walking Worthily</u>
Jesus is resurrected! Who cares. What difference does it make? Not the reaction you expected from me? I am simply speaking for the majority of Christendom. Think about it, unless it is the traditional yearly time to remember, how important is the resurrection? Church buildings are filled to capacity one week, and the returnees can hear the echoes seven days later. Did the resurrection message have an effect on them? Did it change their lives? Is the resurrection solely a past historical fact, or does it have significance—daily significance—to me personally, here and now and later? Does it affect my walk today? If I understand grace, it will.

There is so much anguish in this world. Through His resurrection, Jesus will resurrect those who are His with a new immortal body. End of physical anguish. End of sin's curse on my body. That's grace. Jesus delivers us from fear in this life and fear in the next. End of emotional anguish. That's grace. Should that lift up our spiritual walk?

People living before the New Covenant believed in the resurrection and afterlife with only a shadow of knowledge. "Is there life after death?" one might query (Job 14.14). "I believe there is," comes the answer, but doubt and fear ride together. Jesus came and shared "in flesh and blood, He Himself likewise also partook of the same, that through death He might render powerless him who had the power of death, that is, the devil; and might deliver those who through fear of death were subject to slavery all their lives" (Heb. 2.14–15). The resurrection is as essential as the incarnation. Both Jesus' life and "re-life" change the way I live. If I understand grace.

How does Jesus deliver us from the fear of death? Let's look at Matthew 16.18. "I also say to you that you are Peter, and upon this rock I will build My church; and the gates of Hades will not overpower it." In the past, I had a very defensive and passive interpretation of this passage—hades was on the attack; Jesus was being attacked. That is totally wrong! Jesus attacked the gates of Hades. Hades is under attack. Hades is defending itself against the assault of Jesus! There are two possible aggressive interpretations.

One possibility is that Jesus is outside the gates, tearing them down and releasing all the inhabitants inside, removing the power of death. A second possibility is that when Jesus died, He passed through the gates of Hades as its prisoner—a prisoner of death—but in His resurrection, He tore down the gates from the inside, leading to freedom a score of spiritual soldiers. I prefer this latter view, and it harmonizes with Ephesians 4.8, "When He ascended on High, He led captive a host of captives."

We will one day be on the inside (precluding Jesus' return first) of the gates of Hades. Not a pleasant thought. Death is contrary to grace for death is the consequence of sin. Jesus is coming to get us, and we are marching out! We know that because we understand grace!

We see Paul expanding on the graceful effects of the resurrection in Colossians. We can call this "the resurrection power of the renovated image." Let's begin with reliving the gospel of grace:

- Dead in transgression (2.13)—old life
- Died with Christ (2.20)
- Buried with Christ in baptism (2.12)
- Raised with Christ (2.12, 3.1)—new life

Notice how the following actions help me to walk worthily; notice what the effect is of me being spiritually resurrected now:

- Keep seeking (v. 1)
- Set your mind (v. 2)
- Put to death sin (vv. 5–9)
- Put on new and renewing self (v. 10)

Death and resurrection; putting off and putting on—the putting off and putting on of vv. 8–10 teaches us that we are alive in Christ. Some, however, (and that means too many) are still living in the grave. We now have an oxymoron: "the alive are dead." This is the opposite of the "occultist" zombies — "the dead are alive." As foolish as it sounds to think of zombies, it is equally foolish for a Christian to still live in sin. Too often, I am the foolish one.

We were formed in God's image and deformed from God's image by our sin. But through Jesus Christ, we can be transformed into God's image. After all, isn't Jesus the image of God? That's the power of understanding grace. Walk worthy!

Understand Jesus is Fully First

Colossians 1.18: "So that He Himself might come to have first place in everything."

<u>Filled With Knowledge</u>
All the work of God was to glorify Jesus. All the work of Jesus was to glorify God. Harmony. The first-born of all creation, the first-born from the dead, is to have first place in everything. Everything in the Old Covenant looked forward to Christ. And now, everything in my life must look backward to God's grace on the cross. Everything leading up to the birth of Christ happened for the birth of Christ. Every detail, every movement had to coincide with Jesus' coming. If anything interfered in that, it could not happen. That's the message of grace.

And yet, even though Jesus came to have first place in everything, did everything in His life happen without pain and sacrifice? There's a lesson in there for us and our attitudes and expectations.

Walking Worthily

If God planned for His Son to have first place, what should my plan be? Jesus is supreme. There is no one above Him, no one more important. If everything God did was to glorify Jesus, then what about our lives and us? Does Jesus have first-place? Is Jesus supreme in:

- Our thinking
- Our worship
- Our work
- Our families
- Our leisure activities
- Our computer time
- Our job choice
- Our living situations
- Our time with our friends
- Our use of our money
- Our use of our time
- Our relationships with others
- Our ambitions
- Our dreams

Understanding grace causes me to grow because it affects every aspect of my life. Walk worthy!

Understand Jesus Is Fully Divine

Colossians 1.19: "For it was the Father's good pleasure for all the fullness to dwell in Him."

Filled With Knowledge

Again, Jesus' divinity is affirmed. Earlier, the text said that Jesus is the image of God. This time, the emphasis is on that image being full even while encased in flesh. God in the flesh. God incarnate. So easy to say. Harder to believe. Difficult to explain. Impossible to understand.

Fullness, not partiality, is the point. Did Jesus retain His Divine attributes while He was incarnated? If God, unlike man, does not have any nonessential attributes, then Jesus could not have divested even one attribute and remain the Divine person He was. Each essential attribute is what makes Jesus a Divine person, just as each essential attribute is what makes me a human person. If Deity is His attributes, then a Divine person cannot exist minus those characteristics. If Deity is not His attributes, then the Divine person could exist without ever having had them.

For in Him, all the fullness of Deity dwells in bodily form (Col. 2.9). My worship is not only directed toward God the Father, but also to Jesus the Son.

Walking Worthily

Everything associated with Jesus and ultimately our salvation pleased God. Pleasing God should be our ultimate goal (1.10). So easy to say. Harder to do. Difficult to accomplish. Impossible to perfect. Easier if I am filled with the fullness of Christ. Walk worthy!

Understand Jesus is Fully Savior

Colossians 1.20: "And through Him to reconcile all things to Himself, having made peace through the blood of His cross; through Him, I say, whether things on earth or things in heaven."

Filled With Knowledge

Reconciliation is "a change of enmity into friendship" (Barclay); "the restoration of a proper relationship between two parties." These two definitions teach us two glorious truths: (1) God is our friend, not our enemy—if we are saved. If we are not, then He is the worst enemy we could have. (2) God never intended for us to be enemies; our proper relationship is one of friendship.

Another point must be understood from this verse concerning reconciliation. Although we are the enemy, God reaches out and down to us. God is not reconciled to us, but rather we are to him (2 Cor. 5.19).

The enmity that has existed between Creator and creation can now be ended. This cessation is not a truce, but a complete victory. Just as the first creation came into existence through Jesus, so too does the new creation.

Walking Worthily

The greatest practical application is freedom. We have freedom from our sin, freedom from Satan, but most practically, we have freedom from ourselves. What I mean by that is freedom from self-doubt, freedom from self-condemnation, freedom from self-salvation, which is an acknowledgment that while we cannot be saved without our works, we cannot be saved by our works.

Do you remember what I said about "although we are the enemy, God reaches out and down"? That is a wonderful practical lesson for us all. We need to make the first step in reconciliation with others, whether they are believers or not, even when we have not done wrong. In doing so, we are following the example of God. Isn't that enough motivation? Walk worthy!

At the beginning of this chapter, we emphasized the power of asking questions. Here is the summation question: How can all this knowledge of the grace of God change us? The answer is by living what we know! Easier said than done, I know. But impossible to live, unless I first know—unless I first understand grace—and the grace-giver.

Do we understand grace?

Questions

1. How did Jesus get people's attention?

2. How can we better understand grace? (hint, theme of Colossians)

3. Filling ourselves with the knowledge of Jesus Christ should lead us to do what?

4. What should be understood when we "understand" grace?

5. What is the definition of the word "understood" as found in Colossians 1.6?

6. After reading the Amplified version of Colossians 1.6, write in your own words your understanding of this verse.

_____

_____

_____

_____

7. How does what we believe about Jesus change and affect our behavior every day?

_____

_____

8. From the book of Colossians, what things should we specifically learn about Jesus? Col. 1.15-20

_____

_____

_____

_____

9. Many scholars believe Colossians 1.15-20 is an ancient what?

_____

10. What two sections can Colossians 1.15-20 be divided into?

_____

_____

11. In Col. 1.9-10, what is the "theological" section and what is the "practical"?

12. Explain the two diametrically opposed extremes that we see in Christianity today, "academic" and "better felt than told".

13. What are some other scriptures that repeat the message of Jesus being the image of the invisible God as found in Colossians 1.15a?

14. In Colossians 3.10, we find we are being renewed to a true knowledge, according the image of the One who created us. From this, what should be our goal?

15. How can understanding grace make visible the invisible God?

16. Jesus is the first-born, Col. 1.15b. Many misunderstand this verse and state that Jesus was created. What is the only way our grace-giver Jesus was "created"?

_____

_____

17. Why is Jesus over all creation and why is He the first-born?

_____

_____

18. What is made clear in Col. 1.16?

_____

_____

_____

19. What can we learn by understanding Jesus is the Creator? (hint, "Since Christ…")

_____

_____

_____

_____

20. What verse in Colossians 1 tells us that in Jesus "all things hold together"?

_____

21. What comfort can we personally realize in understanding Jesus holds all things together?

_____

_____

22. Read Colossians 1.18, 2.10, and 2.19. Why do some Christians deny Jesus as being Lord and Savior (being Head) and what does this have to do with their misunderstanding of grace?

_____

_____

_____

23. What can we understand about grace from accepting Jesus as our head?

_____

_____

24. What do we learn from Col. 1.18 regarding Jesus being the first-born of the dead?

_____

_____

25. What can we learn from 2 Cor. 5 about our spirits and bodies?

_____

_____

26. How does understanding the Jesus was resurrected and that one day we will be, teach us about grace?

27. How does Col. 2.12, 13, 20 and 3.1 "relive the gospel of grace"?

28. Once spiritually resurrected, how does Col. 3.1-2, 5-10 tell of what I should do to "walk worthily"?

29. How does the misunderstanding of Col. 3.8-10 cause many to be "living in the grave"?

30. How does understanding that Jesus is "fully first" teach us the message of grace?

31. In what ways can we personally apply Jesus being first place in our lives?

4

The Grace That Obligates

Romans 5.20–21, 6.1

When I got married, I "died" to my bachelorhood. I told my wife that's why men wear black—the wedding is our funeral. She didn't think it was funny. Furthermore, can you believe that my wife had the audacity to say I couldn't date anymore? What nerve! I am being facetious because we all understand that marriage has moral obligations. Both a relationship in marriage and in Christ has obligations. In marriage, we die to one lifestyle to gratefully live another. In Christ, we die to sin (Rom. 6.2) to live in grace.

Our text will begin with Romans 5.20–21, which serves both as a conclusion to vv.12–19 and an introduction to chapters six and seven. A question to ask when studying this passage is: do too many Christians allow God to free them from the penalty of sin, but not the power of sin? It is the freedom from each of these that obligates us to obey. That's when we experience grace more fully.

Romans 5.20: "The Law came in so that the transgression would increase; but where sin increased, grace abounded all the more."

Does this sound fair? It's like saying to a drowning man, "Would you like to supersize your drink?" or giving a sick man medicine to make him sicker. Would you want to take that kind of medicine? And yet:

> The wise physician often gives medicine to bring the disease from within to the surface, and make it abound, so to speak, with a view of driving away the disorder, and so enabling health to reign in the system of his patient. (Lyth in Coffman, 213)

Medically that might be true, but I think the emphasis in Romans 5.20 is slightly different. Maybe this is naïve of me, but I think the lesson is very simple. God wanted to prove the point that we need Him. The more we fail to obey God's laws, the more we should realize we need God.

Let's do a self-examination of our views on how much we need God:

Question 1: Could we keep one law perfectly? Are we any better than Adam and Eve? Have we ever thought that we would not have made the same mistake as the original sinners? Have we mocked their weakness? Come on now, haven't we thought with incredulity, "Couldn't they obey just that one little command? Don't eat! One little law, and they blew it. That's just pitiful!" That kind of thinking is hypocritical and wrong. How often have we also blown one little law?

Eating the forbidden fruit is something I can't say without reservation and hesitation that I would not have done. Not to be flippant, but how many of us have failed on diets? Food seems to be the downfall of most of us. In fact . . .

Confession time. I just ate a huge piece of cheesecake (OK, two pieces stuck together) after eating a small dinner (I am on a diet after all). But that's OK. I prepared myself for success tomorrow by eating the last of the cheesecake tonight. Tomorrow I shall not eat any more cheesecake!

Rationalization . . . add that to my list of sins to work on.

Question 2: Could we keep any law perfectly? Some Jews in the time of Jesus thought salvation could be accomplished by keeping at least one law perfectly. If that were so, which law would you choose? Would you select a negative or positive command? Would your choice be a "never" or an "always" command? Can you name one law you have kept perfectly? Admittedly, I have never committed certain sins. I have never murdered anyone. But I have been wrongfully angry, and we know what Jesus said regarding that (Matt. 5.21–22). Maybe my standard of law-keeping is less than holy. Upon further reflection, then, maybe I haven't perfectly kept even one law. That is depressing.

More laws simply prove that I need God and His grace. Maybe the purpose of more laws is to cover more people because God wrote enough laws to cover each and every one of us.

Laws are necessary even in the covenant of grace. Why? Because laws describe and differentiate between righteousness and sin.

> Romans 7.7: What shall we say then? Is the Law sin? May it never be! On the contrary, I would not have come to know sin except through the Law; for I would not have known about coveting if the Law had not said, "YOU SHALL NOT COVET."

Laws can't save, but they can keep us saved through obedience. However, who obeys perfectly? We aren't saved by our works, but we can't be saved without works (Rom. 1.5; 6.16; 15.18; 16.19,26). Add that to the paradoxes of Christianity. And yet, if I had to choose being saved by law or grace, no doubt I have more confidence in God than myself . . . usually. I struggle balancing the obligation to obey and the perfection of obedience. I struggle with trusting my obedience more than trusting God's grace. I keep failing. I keep needing God's grace. I keep needing to be reminded I need God's grace. Ironically, God's laws keep me realizing I need God's grace.

> The whole point here being a thrust against those who feel that real help is given by law. Here's a man struggling with the first three commands and losing. He calls on God for help, and God gives him four more commands. He groans even more now and asks for further help, and he gets three more commandments. What the man needs is to recognize his need of grace since he has already condemned himself. If he is slow in recognizing that, then adding laws to law will cause sin to multiply and convince the man of the impotence of sin" [and law, PDH]. (McGuiggan, 180)

Sometimes the best way we can help those living opposed to God and suffering from their own selves is by letting them sink so low for so long that they hit rock bottom. This is what God has graciously shown us. God gave them over to lusts, degrading passions, and depraved minds (Rom. 1.24,26,28). In this way, the defiant sinner will understand the only way is God's way. Almost drowning is a frightening experience. But no one needs saving in the wading pool. Increased laws prove the need for increased grace.

If you have ever worked with addicts, you know that lesson. I am beginning to think that we are all addicts, which is why we keep sinning. Some of us are addicted to illegal sins and others to socially acceptable sins. Letting people sink, that's tough love, and it's tough to do, and tough on both those showing love and those being shown the door. Addicts need to realize that they can't make it on their own. We all need to realize that. God's laws keep reminding me I need God's grace.

To teach sinners this eternal lesson, Paul said that God chose to increase the number of laws. Instead of increasing the laws so that there are more transgressions, what if God takes away some laws so that we will not be so sinful? That would make things easier, but would it make us better? Remember Adam and Eve.

Such thinking is actually advocated socially. People argue that we should remove the laws banning certain illegal victimless activities because people are breaking them anyway. They say that if we legalize drugs, the crime rate will go down. Can't argue with that logic since you can't break a law if there isn't a law to break. Obviously, if we legalize murder, the crime rate will again go down. But just because fewer crimes are committed, does that mean people are better citizens? Not hardly, if the standard of what is acceptable has been lowered. Therefore, if we had fewer laws from God, that would not make us better citizens of His kingdom. God has given us the only means that can forge righteous living—law and grace, properly understood. Laws teach me righteousness. Grace teaches me I am not righteous. Grace teaches me righteousness beyond laws.

Fewer laws to create pseudo-holiness are also advocated religiously. While there are fewer laws in the New Covenant as compared to the Old, some claim we are not under any type of law except the law of love (1 Cor. 9.21).

Problem is folks, how can sinful people who keep sinning selfishly decide on their own how to show love selflessly? That cannot be done because we need God to show us how through His laws and grace. Laws are the expression of love.

> Matthew 22.37–40: And He said to him, "You shall love the Lord your God with all your heart, and with all your soul and with all your mind." This is the great and foremost commandment. The second is like it, "You shall love your neighbor as yourself." On these two commandments depend the whole Law and the Prophets.

What the scriptures teach is that we are not under law in the sense that perfect law-keeping is not our justifier; grace is our justifier. Even my obedience is not what makes me righteous ultimately. It is the God whom I am obeying that accomplishes that feat. Every time I obey, it is God crediting me because my faith is in Him and not in my obedience. That, however, does not take away our responsibility of obeying God. If we are not under any law, then we never can sin! And if we can never sin then we have no need for God's grace! And if we have no need for God's grace, then we have no need for God!

Listen very carefully: all this means is that my justification (i.e., forgiveness) by grace can motivate and obligate me to not sin. What was the cost of grace? Jesus' crucifixion. Therefore, needing forgiveness is itself a supernatural thought. Where sin increased/*pleonazo*, grace abounded/*huperperisseuo* all the more because grace is more powerful than any sin. How so? Grace is from God; sin is from man. Grace comes from divine love; sin comes from a warped love of self.

Romans 5.21: "So that, as sin reigned in death, even so, grace would reign through righteousness to eternal life through Jesus Christ our Lord."

The power words in this verse are not "sin," "death," "grace," and "righteousness." They are "as" and "even so." Just "as" sin leads to death (and no Bible-believing person could deny that), "even so" grace leads to righteousness"—not more sinfulness.

- Grace obligates and persuades me to live righteously. Jesus is my

King, not death. My allegiance to my King and His laws is just one of the paradoxes of grace since we are not under law.

- Grace obligates us even more to obey than trying to save ourselves through perfection.
- Grace obligates us to live a righteous life because there is grace when I fail to live righteously.
- Grace obligates us to live morally and righteously because of the cost of grace.
- Grace obligates us to live ethically and lawfully because of what it means to be saved by grace – to die to sin. To die to sin is not being dead inwardly; it is being alive to God.

Romans 6.1: "What shall we say then? Are we to continue in sin so that grace may increase?"

"Yes, yes, yes, and a thousand times yes?" No! I can't imagine Paul saying something like that. But, if grace abounds even more when sin increases (Rom. 5.20), isn't my obligation as a Christian to sin even more in order to give God the glory? While Paul wouldn't say that, apparently someone was—and apparently some were listening. The easy way is often the popular way.

So what are the obligations of grace? That's what Paul's question is about. What does grace obligate me to do and be? The Russian monk Rasputin, for example, claimed he was doing God a favor by living bawdily: "Just think how much grace God could bestow on me," he might argue (Yancy, 27).

To continue in sin does not glorify God. Yet somehow, the Roman Christians were battling a damningly wrong theology about being saved by grace. They wrongly believed that not being under law meant obedience is unnecessary and even contrary to grace. Someone had started to convince them that being saved by grace obligated them to sin more often.

Before debunking their argument, let me ask the question, why would someone teach that? We could get philosophical and say that antinomianism is part of Gnosticism. Did your eyes just glaze over? Part of me would suggest that it is natural to want to sin, and therefore trying to justify it theologically is to be expected.

But another part of me can't help but wonder how strange this doctrine of grace was to the world, and still is to the world, and even to some of us Christians. Paul claimed he was not ashamed of the gospel (Rom. 1.16). Were some Christians ashamed? Grace is contrary to human logic and fairness.

I doubt I will ever get my mind fully wrapped around grace in its totality. Sadly, if there is one topic that has been controversial over the centuries, it is grace. People have used grace to excuse the sinner for sinning, instead of forgiving the sinner for sinning. I will never forget hearing a preacher boast that because he had been saved by grace, he could be committing adultery with an unsaved woman, and both die while sinning. He would go to heaven, and she would go to hell. Folks, that is not grace. That is turning the grace of our God into licentiousness (Jude 1.4). That is not grace, but it is shameful for which someone should be ashamed.

So how could these Roman Christians think believers should sin more because we have been saved by grace? Follow the twisted and yet sinfully appealing logic:

- When I sin by breaking God's law, He provides a way to take away that offense. Is that true? Yes.

- Therefore, the more I sin, the more grace I need. That's true, isn't it? Yes again.

- The more grace I need, the more God's glorious plan can shine. Again who could deny that?

- Therefore, I need to sin more and more so that God can forgive more and more! Uhhh?

- Therefore, I glorify God by sinning?! No! Wrong! Damningly wrong! This is a case where simple logic is simply wrong . . . and not really logical either.

Romans 6.2: "May it never be! How shall we who died to sin still live in it?"

Peter Leithart had this apt analogy:

> If grace comes flooding in precisely where sin has been most abundant, perhaps we should stay in the place where sin abounds so we can gain full experience of grace. Paul rejects that reasoning. It is just as absurd to stay where sin abounds as it was for Israel to want to go back to Egypt. Once Israel had passed through the water, there was no going back. And every Christian has passed through the water, leaving behind the Egypt where Death and Sin reign and entering into a new world where Life and Righteousness have the throne. (www.leithard.com)

Grace necessitates death, both Christ's and ours. In reading that we have died to sin (6.2), Paul's emphasis in his theology of grace is not that it is mechanically impossible for Christians to sin. I wish we had received some spiritual operation performed by the Holy Spirit, removing not only our past sin but even the ability or desire to sin. I wish it just wasn't "in us" anymore to sin.

But if such were true, then why does Paul feel compelled to not only discuss the issue but to disarm the false teaching? Ironically, if it became impossible for Christians to sin, that would betray the need for grace after salvation by creating a salvation based upon perfection. We could save ourselves because we never sin anymore. After all, if we no longer sin, then don't we become perfect? Yet, reality is what it is. Saved people do sin. I do. You do. Those who say Christians never sin are, to quote one of my daughters, "oblivious to the obvious." Those who say Christians never sin just did.

> 1 John1.8: If we say that we have no sin, we are deceiving ourselves and the truth is not in us.

Thankfully, salvation by grace is not based upon our perfect obedience either before or after salvation. Law is so weak if we have sinned even once, obeying all the other laws does not have the legal power to forgive. That is not the function of law. That is why we are not under law (6.14). Law cannot save the lost. I cannot make up for running a red light by obeying the speed limit. Think that argument would work with the local police department?

"Excuse me officer, didn't you see me drive at the speed limit right after I ran the red light? That's got to count for something, right?"

Making up for sin by obeying other laws would be akin to washing with dirt.

> Isaiah 64.6: For all of us have become like one who is unclean, And all our righteous deeds are like a filthy garment; And all of us wither like a leaf, And our iniquities, like the wind, take us away.

Does dying to sin mean we no longer have the ability to sin? Does it mean we are no longer attracted to sin? Truly, I wish sin no longer fascinated me. Personally, there are several levels of attraction, detraction, and distraction to sin.

The first group of sins is those that repulse me. Admittedly, I can't ever picture myself committing certain spiritual atrocities. And yet, it is difficult thinking of even one single sin that I don't know of someone who committed it. Those sinners need God's grace, and some have received it. But they still struggled after receiving God's grace. Homosexuality, child molestation, murder, drugs —all have no appeal to me. Never in my wildest imagination could I ever see myself addicted to drugs, especially heroin. I hate needles. Yet, whoever plans on becoming a drug addict? You want to know what repulses me about drugs and alcohol: losing control. It is hard enough to allow God to manage my life, so giving control over to drugs is totally unattractive and unfathomable. Dying to sin is giving power over my life to God. Giving control of my life to God is living by grace. Here's a paradox for you: self-control (and its many synonyms) is an oft-recurring theme in the Bible. Why? Because the paradox of self-control is the essence of Christianity. What is the paradox of self-control? We must possess self-control in order to give up self-control to God, who will then control our self. How can I give to God what I do not have? After I give away myself, only then can I truly have control of self by not keeping control of self.

> Luke 17.33: Whoever seeks to keep his life will lose it, and whoever loses his life will preserve it.

I am learning that true happiness is removing contradictions and then replacing them with God's paradoxes in my life.

A second group of sins is trespasses that appear beyond the realm of reality for me, yet don't necessarily repulse me. I don't do them, but I can understand them, at least to some degree. And admittedly, knowing that bothers me. How many of us have friends who have committed adultery, or fight addiction to pornography? I have certain safeguards, such as never meeting or studying with a woman alone. I can't ever imagine committing this sin against my wife and my God . . . I love them too much, and I could not handle the guilt. But then I remember David . . . and David was a man after God's own heart. In one moment, David didn't live the obligations of grace.

A third category of trespasses is the one that plagues me every once in a while. I fight them off for a while, and then I receive a respite, only for them to return. Self-pity fighting against pride—what a schizophrenic sinner I can be!

Finally, there are sins that seem a daily struggle. Do you want to know what they are? Too bad! My God knows them, and that is shameful enough. I know all too well that I have the ability to sin. I keep proving it to myself and others—especially my family. I open myself up to you in this self-diagnosis to demonstrate that dying to sin does not mean losing the ability to sin. But beyond personal experience, I know for certain that this text is not teaching that dying to sin means no longer having the ability to sin. Why? Because the same phrase is used of Jesus:

> Romans 6.10: For the death that He died, He died to sin once for all; but the life that He lives, He lives to God.

Did Jesus have the ability to sin, and then lose it? Could it mean an inborn inclination to sin had been removed? That cannot be, or else consistency would require us to say Jesus was born with sin. Again, the text says that Jesus died to sin (6.10). What about repentance? Does being dead to sin mean we have repented? Not in this context because, again, Christ is also said to have "died to sin" (6.10).

What does it mean then? How about not allowing sin to rule over me because I have entered into a union with Christ where He is my master and sin is not? How about making a mental and moral choice as to whose side I am on? How about submitting in slavery to righteousness and not to sin? Those ideas are found within the text (6.9,14,16,17–19). Those ideas match Jesus. He did not serve sin; He served His master, the Father. Paul is presenting a moral and personal impetus for obeying, not a mechanical inability to sin. Obedience wouldn't mean much if I couldn't disobey.

But maybe, more importantly, grace's moral obligation to obey is even stronger than a legal obligation. My motivation for not sinning is not law, but grace. The import of the Holy Spirit's teaching is that Christians have made a moral choice contrary to living immorally. Three times in this chapter, it is stated that Christians are dead or have died, unto sin (vv. 2,7,11). How are we Christians today succeeding in living out our choice of grace-living?

Listen to the next analogy:

> To help Paul's image sink in, I like to picture two dogs. One is a frisky pup from Pet Palace who wags his tail and licks whoever proffers a hand. The other is a dog on the highway that has been flattened by a truck. Which has more appeal, the road-kill dog or the Pet Palace puppy? The answer is obvious, and to Paul, the solution to the theological dilemma is equally obvious. Sin has the stench of death about it. Why would any choose "wickedness" over "righteousness." (Yancy, 28)

Sin is that dead dog! But the problem is that sin doesn't always look like road-kill dogs. That means the devil has convinced us, by mentally and spiritually confusing us, to scrape that dead dog off the pavement, and take it home! Christians living in sin is a dead dog theology.

Romans 6.3: "Or do you not know that all of us who have been baptized into Christ Jesus have been baptized into His death?"

Whatever this baptism is, it is undeniably into Christ and into His death. We have died to sin and died with Christ. Whatever this baptism is, all of Paul's readers had gone through it. Our baptism has moral and ethical ramifications. Our baptism obligates us.

What is this baptism into Christ and His death?

Baptism is a work of God, not a work of man (Col. 2.11–13). Therefore, to believe it is required is not contrary to being saved by grace. God required Jesus to die, and God requires me to die, too. Think: if grace requires me to die to sin, to live morally, ethically, and righteously, which is trusting and obeying God, why would it be contrary to grace to require obedience in baptism? If my baptism obligates me to live morally, then don't I have a moral obligation to be baptized? Baptism is the reenactment of that grace-life.

Baptism is when we receive grace, not how. How we receive grace is through Jesus' death, burial, and resurrection. How we receive grace is through faith. But doesn't the Sovereign God of grace who freely chooses to give us grace have the right to decide when He will deliver us from sin through His grace? To say no denies God's sovereignty.

Baptism is an immersion both in water and the Spirit (Jn. 3.5). I am buried in water because baptism is my tomb. Baptism is also an immersion in the Holy Spirit because baptism is my new birth. Both happen together because I must first die before I can be born again. My burial through immersion into Christ's death is just as real as Christ's burial in the tomb. I cannot witness, and be a witness, of immersion in the Spirit. So both water and the Spirit are needed. Water is my grave, not the Holy Spirit. The Holy Spirit is my resurrection out of my grave. While neither water nor the Spirit is mentioned in this text, both dying and living are.

Baptism was a death, a realization and declaration of personal death—a death in sin and a death to sin. Paul's point is simple and yet striking—how can we sin to the glory of God if we died to sin to the glory of God? How can we sin so that grace may abound if we died to sin so that grace may abound? My baptism says I joined with Christ in His death against sin. My baptism says I joined with Christ in His cause. My baptism says I personally made a choice, a moral choice, and an obligated choice. Paul's readers had been baptized into Christ, which means they had been baptized into His death.

> We were baptized into his death. And what kind of death was that? It was a death caused by sin at the hands of sinners! It was a death that was intended to atone for sin! It was a once-for-all death to sin! And if we entered into union with such a death, could we continue to live in sin? That would be a moral contradiction. Did teaching like Paul's lead (logically) to a life of continuance in sin? Not at all. The

logic of his teaching would be a hatred of that which slew the Master; a longing to have that sin covered and appeased for and a decisive severance from sin. If a person enters into union with Christ, he endorses all that Christ endorses and repudiates all that Christ rejects. (McGuiggan, 193)

Romans 6.4: "Therefore we have been buried with Him through baptism into death, so that as Christ was raised from the dead through the glory of the Father, so we too might walk in newness of life."

The death, burial, and resurrection of Christ—taken as a single event—is a historical fact. It is also the method of grace (1 Pet. 3.21). If I am to die, be buried, and be resurrected with Him, then Jesus must have died, been buried, and was resurrected. Jesus died, was buried, and then was resurrected to give grace; therefore, I die, am buried, and I am resurrected to receive grace. Every time someone is baptized, they are reenacting and verifying the historicity of the gospel of Jesus and the method God used to grant us grace. Baptism is not only connected to grace. It is a powerful apologetic for the whole story of grace. Our immersion into water displays the historical burial and resurrection of Jesus.

The story of grace is not a death, resurrection, and then a burial. The story of grace is not a new birth and then a death. Baptism is a symbol but not a symbol of burying the born again! Jesus died, was buried, and was then resurrected to give me grace. Therefore, I reenact the story of grace by dying to sin, being buried with Christ, and then God resurrecting me out of my tomb to live dead to sin with Christ.

Most are aware that the word baptize itself means immersion. However, when reading the quote below, focus on the implications of being immersed:

> Immersed translates a form of the Greek word "baptizo," usually transliterated "baptized." The root meaning of "baptizo" is "dip, soak, immerse, into a liquid so that what is dipped takes on the qualities of what it has been dipped in—such as cloth in dye or leather in tanning solution".... This is why being immersed into the Messiah (v. 3) is equated with being united with him (v. 5). (Stern, 373)

So when I am immersed, I am immersed with Christ, taking on His characteristics, His purposes, His goals, and His allegiance. Christ's death was for grace; my baptism is for grace. Also, since all of this talk of baptism is connected to the grace of God, we are affirming this grace in our lives by our submission to be buried in baptism. We often look for ways to convince people of the necessity of baptism. Paul here gives us one. We need to be baptized, that is buried because we are dead! That brings us to the question, who is baptism for? Please understand this is asking the same question as, "Who is grace for?"

To further answer the question who is baptism for, let me temporarily move away from our text. Let's make an analogy involving the concept of death, burial, and resurrection, all concepts within Romans 6. Let's look at another death, burial (at least preparation for it), and resurrection.

In Acts 9.36–41, we have the account of Tabitha, who fell sick and died; and when they had washed her body, they laid it in an upper room. Following her death and the washing of her body, Peter sent them all out and knelt down and prayed, and turning to the body, he said, "Tabitha, arise." And she opened her eyes, and when she saw Peter, she sat up. And he gave her his hand and raised her up; and calling the saints and widows, he presented her alive.

According to Jewish ritual, a dead body comes into contact with water twice:

- *Rechitzah*: the body is washed carefully. As all blood must be buried along with the deceased, any open bleeding is stopped. The body is thoroughly cleaned of dirt, body fluids, and solids, and anything else that may be on the skin. All jewelry is removed.

- *Taharah*: the body is purified with water, either by immersion in a mikvah or by pouring a continuous stream in a prescribed manner (i.e., covering the entire body, PDH). The term *taharah* is used to refer both to the overall process of burial preparation, and to the specific step of ritual purification. (www.wikipedia.com, Bereavement in Judaism)

Which washing is being described by Luke in Acts 9.37 is unclear to me. Maybe he wasn't trying to be specific. The fact that a washing is mentioned implies that the whole process was followed, which would include both washings.

The word for "washed" is *louo* and is a generic word for washing whether by a full bath (Jn. 13.10), of wounds (Acts 16.33), for a Christian's washing in baptism (Heb. 10.22), or of the dead (Acts 9.37). Most cultures, like the Jews, had the practice of washing the deceased's body. While there might be many different cultural reasons for washing a dead body, they all have something in common—the body is dead. I'm not trying to be flippant, but rather poignant. Dead bodies were washed. But why?

> "As he came, so shall he go," says Ecclesiastes. Just as a newborn child is immediately washed and enters this world clean and pure, so he who departs this world must be cleansed and made pure through the religious ritual called *taharah* (purification).
>
> The taharah is performed by the Chevra Kadisha (the Holy Society, i.e., the Burial Society), consisting of Jews who are knowledgeable in the area of traditional duties and can display proper respect for the deceased. In addition to the physical cleansing and preparation of the body for burial, they also recite the required prayers asking Almighty G-d for forgiveness for any sins the deceased may have committed, and praying that the All-Merciful may guard him and grant him eternal peace. (www.chabad.org/library/article_cdo/aid/281546/jewish/Taharah-Preparation-of-the-Remains.htm)

The Jewish culture of immersing the dead body in water, in the *mikvah*, was an appeal for forgiveness for the dead. Such an appeal would be a work of man, not God. But since I believe baptism is a work of God, I wonder if this might help some understand the place God has placed baptism within His plan for saving us. Is baptism for those who have already received grace or for those who need it? Is baptism before or after salvation? Is baptism for the lost or for the saved? Is baptism for the dead or the living?

As there was culturally a washing of the physical filth from the physically dead, baptism is itself a washing of the spiritual filth from the spiritually dead. "Now why do you delay? Get up and be baptized, and wash [*apolouo*] away your sins, calling on His name" (Acts 22.16). Sins are our filth. Being dead in sin—and you were dead in your trespasses and sins (Eph. 2.1)—God requires us to wash our dead bodies in baptism. Our washing (*rechitzah*), purification (*taharah*), and burial are one and the same—a burial in the water, a burial in and with Christ.

> 1 Peter 3.21: Corresponding to that, baptism now saves you—not the removal of dirt from the flesh, but an appeal to God for a good conscience—through the resurrection of Jesus Christ,

Baptism submitted to in faith is when we receive grace; Christ's resurrection is how we receive grace. Our baptism is more than a cultural ritual, a family ceremony, a public announcement, and more than just a symbol. Baptism is an admission and declaration that I am dead. I am dead in sin, from sin, and because of sin. My body was the instrument of much of my sin. I wash and purify the body because it is dead. Dead bodies are cleansed. Baptism is for the dead.

But I wonder if there could be more? Why did the Jews wash the deceased's body? The answer is for the same reason they buried the dead. The same reason Jesus was buried. The washing of the dead in Judaism was done in looking forward to the resurrection. Resurrection was not just a Christian belief, but a Jewish one, too.

> One of the most important elements of a proper Jewish burial is the Tahara, preparing the body by the Chevra Kaddisha for its final rest, until the Resurrection of the Dead in the era of Moshiach. (www.chabad.org/library/article_cdo/aid/367843/jewish/The-Taharah.htm)

Also, consider the following:

> In his treatise on the resurrection of the flesh, Tertullian makes an intriguing connection between the phenomenology of baptism and the resurrection of the body. Baptism, he points out, is a corporeal rite, and this washing of the body points to a resurrection of the body: "unless it were a bodily resurrection, there would be no pledge secured through this process of a corporeal baptism." The soul, he argues, is not "sanctified by the baptismal bath." Rather, the sanctification of the soul comes through the "answer," an apparent allusion to 1 Peter 3:21 (ch 38). I'm not particularly taken with the body/soul problematic that Tertullian introduces here, but the connection of corporeal washing to corporeal

resurrection is important. It is the same connection Paul makes in Rom 6, and there Paul includes the "bodily" practices of the Christian life as part of the death and resurrection achieved in baptism. Perhaps also 1 Corinthians 15:29. (www.leithart.com)

In Romans 6, Paul pictures our death. Instead of dying from sin, he says, "How shall we who died to sin still live in it?" (v.2) He also says, "Therefore we have been buried with Him through baptism into death." (v. 4) Christians have made a choice, a moral choice, a choice of life. This life we live is a resurrected life in these formerly morally dead physical bodies, foreshadowing the final bodily resurrection on the last day.

Go ahead and read Romans 6.4–11; it is almost impossible to differentiate the current resurrection of our bodily resurrection through baptism, the morally resurrected life we are to lead now, and our bodily resurrection when Jesus returns. It's as if they are all the same. This is one reason baptism is such a powerful apologetic, not only for the resurrection of Jesus but for our final resurrection when He returns. Our present baptism reaches back to the historical Jesus and forward to the returning Jesus. When we are baptized, we not only look backward to our sins. We look forward to our resurrection. Baptism is for the dead and those who will live again.

Now let's return to our Romans text. As we can see, contrary to grace is the desire to live a life dedicated to ourselves, to sin, and to Satan. So if we didn't want to live the life of grace, why were we ever baptized? That is what Paul is asking the Romans. That is something we can ask an erring Christian. Why did they ever want to receive God's grace? The receiving of God's grace through the resurrection of Christ tells God we want to live for Him. Grace obligates me to live for Christ. Through our choice of allegiance, we have been raised through the glory of the Father. One might expect the text to say power instead of glory, but that is not the case. Why does Paul say it was God's glory that raised Jesus? Personally, I believe it is one of the most important words in this text. Some believe it is synonymous with power, as in glorious power. Others believe it encompasses all of God's attributes. I believe that, although the word glory/*doxa* is used in different ways in Romans, there is also one way that it is repeatedly used (5.1–2, 9.22–23, 15.7). God's glory is connected to God's grace. God is to be glorified, and God is filled with glory because of His grace. God saving us through our being buried and resurrected with Jesus is to God's glory. Our baptism is an act of God, not of man. Our baptism is an act of glory. Our baptism is an act of grace. We are to live glorious lives. We are to live in and for God's glorious grace. Don't we owe God that?

Romans 6.5: "For if we have become united with Him in the likeness of His death, certainly we shall also be in the likeness of His resurrection."

If we died to sin (v.2), we have no choice but to live to God (Acts 2.31–32). This is where Paul has been going all along. Have we truly been resurrected? The answer can only be yes if we have first truly died. We can't be resurrected unless we are first dead. Being raised out of baptism is only a resurrection if we were dead when buried in baptism. Not only am I obligated to live for God after receiving grace, I am obligated to die in order to receive His grace.

Romans 6.6: "Knowing this, that our old self was crucified with Him, in order that our body of sin might be done away with, so that we would no longer be slaves to sin."

The best way to describe the "old self" is to simply call it "me." It is not some inner, inherent disposition to sin. It is me. This includes, if not superimposes, sins not only of the overt fleshly nature but also of pride. Whenever I put myself first, I am forgetting the motivation and obligation of grace.

How are we crucified? Not literally, since it was Christ and only Christ who could atone for sins. Not figuratively, for in this text, Jesus is neither a figure for me nor am I a figure for Jesus. The answer is spiritually—morally—ethically. I am crucified by choice . . . just as Jesus was crucified by choice.

Judicially, the man who sins should die. Human beings do not have the power to die for themselves since our sacrifice would be a defiled sacrifice. However, I am to crucify my old self, my body of sin, as part of Christ's sacrifice. My body is defiled and not good enough. Since I cannot keep my old self, my old body of sin, and since it is not holy for a sacrifice, I must rid myself of it by attaching, so to speak, my body to Christ's. This is a moral decision.

Crucifixion is a violent death. Sometimes we are so concentrated on the pleasantries and controversies of baptism that we forget what precedes and follows. Using the imagery of Paul, sometimes we emphasize the burial to the neglect of killing the subject first. Are we burying people alive? And then do we forget to resurrect them? Although there is physicality to baptism, the spiritual and ethical cannot be forgotten. The physical mirrors the ethical. Listen carefully and hear what I say, not what I don't say. Although the physicality of baptism can be correctly and scripturally taught from Romans 6, it is the ethical and spiritual side of baptism that Paul is emphasizing. And both the physical and the spiritual aspects of baptism are the gospel in action.

Romans 6.7: "For he who has died is freed from sin."

Please tell me . . . if God's grace freed me from sin, why would I want to continue in sin? If I hated sin enough to be freed from it, I should hate sin enough not to return to it as my master. Too many Christians allow God to free them from the penalty of sin, but not the power of sin. It is the freedom from each that obligates us to obey.

> He does not say "sins" but "sin." He doesn't speak of it as needing forgiveness. He says, "crucified and destroyed." Some folks are just trying to hold down or control this "old man"—"this body of sin." They seem to do a pretty good job of it occasionally. On Sunday, they keep him sort of paralyzed, at least while they are in church, but then later on, perhaps on Monday, they drag him out and rub him down, give him a little camphor and smelling salts, give him a good tonic, use some deodorizing soap, put some face powder on him, and by Wednesday night, he is pretty much alive—in fact, so much so that he objects to going to prayer meeting. He has little or no interest in family worship. He is very touchy and hard to get along with; one must handle him with kid gloves. Paul says there is a way to deal with that old man – he needs to be crucified! (Everest, 42–43)

Romans 6.8: "Now if we have died with Christ, we believe that we shall also live with Him."

The below historical note shows the legality of a vicarious death:

Napoleon's war machine was impressing large numbers into the army; and a young father was about to be inducted. His wife and children were gathered around him in a tearful scene as can be imagined; and, in response to such a pathetic situation, one of the man's neighbors stepped forward and took his place, as the laws and customs of that era allowed. The substitute was killed in battle; and several years later the draft apparatus was again operating in that same village, and the same father was hauled before the board a second time for induction. That time, however, the prospective inductee boldly stepped before the board and produced a parchment, signed by the emperor himself:

This man (name) perished upon the battlefield of Rivoli in the person of his substitute (name).

signed: Napoleon Bonaparte (Coffman, 221–222)

Is the living described in Romans 6.8 our current life or life with Christ in the future resurrection? It could be either one, but as I said before, I find it virtually impossible to differentiate in this passage between our physical resurrection out of baptism, our spiritual resurrection with Christ, and our final resurrection on the last day. The point is the same for all three—death leads to life, or more accurately; our new life requires the death of the old man.

Romans 6.9: "Knowing that Christ, having been raised from the dead, is never to die again; death no longer is master over Him."

The historicity of the death, burial, and resurrection is the basis of both fact and faith. And for us, grace. Everything, especially God's grace, is based upon this knowledge. Deny this resurrection, and we deny God's grace. That is why our immersion is such an apologetic declaration. That is why the resurrection of Christ is such a central doctrine.

To me, this is the key to understanding the phrase "died to sin." We have chosen our Master. As Paul later says in this chapter:

Romans 6.16–18: Don't you know that when you offer yourselves to someone to obey him as slaves, you are slaves to the one whom you obey–whether you are slaves to sin, which leads to death, or to obedience, which leads to righteousness? But thanks be to God that, though you used to be slaves to sin, you wholeheartedly obeyed the form of teaching to which you were entrusted. You have been set free from sin and have become slaves to righteousness.

Romans 6.10: "For the death that He died, He died to sin once for all; but the life that He lives, He lives to God."

Why are we told this? That if Christ died to sin once for all, and if I died with Him, I died to sin once for all—or at least I am supposed to. I never need to be enslaved to sin again because, "where sin increased, grace abounded all the more" (5.20). Which is more powerful, sin or grace?

If I shared with Christ in His resurrection, and in His resurrection, He lives to God, what then is my responsibility? I am obligated by grace to live!

Romans 6.11: "Even so consider yourselves to be dead to sin, but alive to God in Christ Jesus."

This is my responsibility, my obligation, based upon the grace of God, which is guaranteed by the historicity of Jesus' death, burial, and resurrection. My responsibility is to take an inventory, which is the meaning of "consider." We made our decision—now live it!

Romans 6.12: "Therefore do not let sin reign in your mortal body so that you obey its lusts."

How do I do this? By dying to sin! How do I die to sin? By the grace of God! By being motivated morally by the grace of God. Not obeying the body's lust is obeying my resurrected body's Lord. I can only have one king—sin, which is self, or my Savior.

Romans 6.13: "And do not go on presenting the members of your body to sin as instruments of unrighteousness; but present yourselves to God as those alive from the dead, and your members as instruments of righteousness to God."

Romans 6.13 is a summation of what my obligations are—I present myself to God. Mark Twain said about law-keeping, "I suppose there's some reason for keeping rules while you're young, so you'll have enough energy left to break them all when you get old." (in Yancy, p.28). Wrong! Keeping laws is presenting myself to God as alive, as resurrected, as dead to sin.

Romans 6.13 is a summation of why my obligations are not to sin—I am resurrected for righteousness. There is no reason to feel defeated, overwhelmed, or mastered by sin. I will sin, but grace releases me from bondage, both spiritual and emotional.

Romans 6.14: "For sin shall not be master over you, for you are not under law but under grace."

To obey the lusts of the body is to sin, and sin is contrary to the righteous living revealed within God's laws and God's grace. Having broken God's law, the condemnation and requirements of law become my master, beating and scourging me. I cannot get up off my knees and become perfect after I have sinned even once. I don't want the requirement of perfection to be my master. I can't handle law as my master. I need grace. Grace frees me from my imperfections, frees me from the need to be perfect, and frees me from sin and the power of sin. But what grace does not do, and cannot do, is free me from the obligation to live righteously. Isn't righteousness why I want grace?

Paul considers our obligations to live ethical and lawful lives so important that after answering the question, "What shall we say then? Are we to continue in sin so that grace may increase? May it never be!" (Rom. 6.1–2a), he asks the same question almost word for word again. "What then? Shall we sin because we are not under law but under grace? May it never be!" (Rom. 6.15). So, did Paul consider this an important question? Is the answer important?

We have seen Paul use the illustration of death and resurrection. Later in this chapter, he uses the illustration of slaves and masters.

Romans 6.17–18: "But thanks be to God that though you were slaves of sin, you became obedient from the heart to that form of teaching to which you were committed, and having been freed from sin, you became slaves of righteousness."

I am enslaved to that form of teaching, which is the gospel. The death, burial, and resurrection of Jesus is the gospel. I obey the gospel in my life as

I die to sin, am buried in baptism, and am resurrected with Christ to morally live for God. I am God's slave.

Does being saved by grace sound like a lackadaisical life? What does the grace of God obligate me to do?

- Die to sin
- Walk in newness of life
- Be united in Christ's death
- Be united in Christ's resurrection
- Crucify my old self
- Do away with my body of sin
- Not be a slave to sin
- Be freed from sin
- Live with Christ
- Be alive to God
- Not let sin reign in my body
- Present myself to God and righteousness
- Be obedient
- Bear fruit

Our death to sin and life to Christ shows allegiance and obligation. We should no more want to live a life dedicated to death than hug and kiss a dead dog or another man's wife. Grace frees us to live for God, not for ourselves. For us to refuse to die to sin, to prefer to live a sinful life, is to leave Jesus unresurrected, unburied, and unwilling to die for us . . . and that is to leave us without grace.

Questions

1. What causes grace to be multiplied? (Rom. 5.20-21)

2. How are we all like addicts?

3. Why would having fewer laws from God not make us better citizens of His kingdom?

4. What does law and grace together teach us?

5. What would the thinking that we are not under law ultimately lead to?

6. List ways that grace obligates us:

_____

_____

_____

_____

7. What was an obvious wrong that the Roman Christians were being influenced in regards to grace and sin? (Rom. 6.1)

_____

_____

_____

_____

8. How has the topic of grace become controversial over the centuries even from the very beginning of the church?

_____

_____

_____

_____

9. What does Rom. 6.1-11 teach us about grace, sin, and death?

10. What paradox is the essence of Christianity?

11. How does Rom. 6 prove that dying to sin does not mean no longer having the ability to sin (using Jesus as an example)?

12. What verses in Rom. 6 point out that Christians are dead or have died to sin?

13. List scriptures that detail what baptism into Christ and His death means.

14. How does being baptized verify the gospel and the method God uses to grant us grace?

___

15. Using Rom. 6, how does our baptism obligate how we live?

___

16. Rom. 6.4 says Christ was raised from the dead by the glory of the Father. How is God's glory connected to God's grace?

___

17. Using Rom. 6, how does being dead before being buried refute those who teach baptism is done after God's grace is bestowed and being alive in Christ?

_____

_____

_____

18. How does being freed from sin through baptism obligate us to obey God in our lives thereafter?

_____

_____

_____

19. How does us having "died to sin" give us obligations and what are they? (Rom. 6 or other passages)

_____

_____

_____

20. What obligation can grace not do?

_____

_____

5

The Grace That Motivates

2 Corinthians 8–9

To those who appreciate God's grace, what are four words that do not usually, if ever, cross their lips? "Do I have to?" How many children at their own birthday party, sitting in front of a table full of gifts, when told they can now open all their gifts, whine, "Do I have to?" Men, if we asked a woman to marry us and she responded, "Do I have to?" how would we feel? That's not quite the response we were hoping for. God has granted us grace. What is our response? The recurring theme in this chapter is grace received is grace given. Grace motivates even when giving money.

When I was around ten years old, Mike borrowed a dime from me...and never paid me back. Back then, a dime would buy a small box of Milk Duds, my favorite candy, because everything else cost a quarter. Did I mention he never paid me back? My daughters calculated that 10 cents compounded annually at 10 percent for 35 years equals $2.81. Mike now owes me $2.81 .. . and counting.

The sad fact that I remember this whole episode shows the impression it left on my young mind. To this day, I remember standing by a telephone booth yelling at him to pay me back. I even remember his reddish-blonde hair and pointed, freckled face.

Breathe in, breath out, breathe in, breathe out... OK, I'm calm again. Hey Mike, if you are reading this, keep the dime. How gracious of me!

There are two groups of Christians involved in this discussion of grace: the Macedonians and the Corinthians. Which are we more like?

The Macedonian Churches

The Macedonian Christians were filled with grace, and they filled others with grace. They received grace and gave grace. Let's begin with a little background information, both about the Macedonians and about how grace received is grace given.

The Macedonians were motivated to sacrificially give to the needy saints in Jerusalem. They never asked, "Do we have to?" How and why could a church so poor give with so much grace?

The Bereans, Philippians, and Thessalonians were the Macedonians. The grace of God received began before this marvelous example.

> Acts 16:9–10: A vision appeared to Paul in the night: a man of Macedonia was standing and appealing to him, and saying, "Come over to Macedonia and help us." When he had seen the vision, immediately we sought to go into Macedonia, concluding that God had called us to preach the gospel to them.

Knowing the beginning of their experience in receiving grace might help explain their willingness to give grace. Grace received is grace given.

To help us understand how grace motivated the Macedonians and Corinthians in 2 Corinthians 8–9, let's try to understand a woman whom I believe is often misunderstood. I honestly hope our misunderstanding of this mysterious woman is not an indication of our misunderstanding of God's grace and its motivating power.

> Luke 7.36–38: Now one of the Pharisees was requesting Him to dine with him, and He entered the Pharisee's house and reclined at the table. And there was a woman in the city who was a sinner; and when she learned that He was reclining at the table in the Pharisee's house, she brought an alabaster vial of perfume, and standing behind Him at His feet, weeping, she began to wet His feet with her

tears, and kept wiping them with the hair of her head, and kissing His feet and anointing them with the perfume.

Why was this woman crying? What motivated her to "make a scene?" The common answer is that she was a sinner, possibly a prostitute, who desperately desired spiritual purity, and her need for divine love overwhelmed her need for propriety. The common answer is wrong. Keep reading, but remember a theme I will stress throughout this chapter—grace received is grace given.

> Luke 7.39: Now when the Pharisee who had invited Him saw this, he said to himself, "If this man were a prophet He would know who and what sort of person this woman is who is touching Him, that she is a sinner."

Simon is "the Pharisee who did not care to see." He didn't see who Jesus was, what motivated the sinful woman, or his own spiritual need. Jesus is about to prove that He not only knows the woman but Simon as well.

> Luke 7.40–43: And Jesus answered him, "Simon, I have something to say to you." And he replied, "Say it, Teacher." "A moneylender had two debtors: one owed five hundred denarii, and the other fifty. "When they were unable to repay, he graciously forgave them both. So which of them will love him more?" Simon answered and said, "I suppose the one whom he forgave more." And He said to him, "You have judged correctly."

Remember, the parable is designed to illuminate the real-life scenario taking place right before Simon's eyes. In the parable, when does love come? After the debt is graciously forgiven. Why does love come? Because the debt is graciously forgiven. What was common about both debts? Neither could be repaid.

> Luke 7.44–48: Turning toward the woman, He said to Simon, "Do you see this woman? I entered your house; you gave Me no water for My feet, but she has wet My feet with her tears and wiped them with her hair. "You gave Me no kiss; but she, since the time I came in, has not ceased to kiss My feet. "You did not anoint My head with oil, but she anointed My feet with perfume. "For this reason I say to you, her sins, which are many, have been forgiven, for she loved much; but

he who is forgiven little, loves little." Then He said to her, "Your sins have been forgiven."

"Do you see this woman?" I personally think this question is hilarious. Who didn't see this woman? The Pharisee did not see. True reality was contrary to his reality because he had yet to truly see this woman.

Why was this woman crying? What motivated her? Jesus said, "for she loved much (v. 47). Why did she love much? Because she had been forgiven much (v. 47). The common view is that her great love led to great forgiveness. The common view is wrong. Her love did not motivate divine forgiveness. Divine forgiveness motivated her love. "For she loved much (v. 47)," refers to the reason why this Pharisee (and we) should know she was already forgiven. Her love is the effect of grace and forgiveness, not the cause. Her love did not motivate God's forgiveness, but God's forgiveness did motivate her love. Grace received is grace given.

How do we know this? What is the purpose of the parable? It is to demonstrate the result of forgiveness—deep, sacrificial love, and giving as a result of grace. In the parable—remember—love follows forgiveness (vv. 40–43). To say that the woman's love led to her forgiveness is contrary to Jesus' parable. It would not be parabolic for the Master Teacher to leave this parable's point to prove something else, namely, that love precedes forgiveness. The parable proves the reality of the woman's condition. She had already been forgiven before she ever poured out her expensive vial of perfume upon Jesus' head.

Besides this parable of Jesus, there is another reason we know the phrase "for she loved much" does not refer to the reason for her forgiveness. The evidence that she was forgiven is the statement immediately following: he who is forgiven little loves little (v. 47). Is Jesus saying God will only forgive us of our little sins, or only a few sins if we only love Him a little? The point is, our recognition of God's forgiveness and grace in our lives leads to our love. If we think we are a great sinner, we love greatly when forgiven. If we think we are a small sinner, we will only love a little when forgiven.

A third reason we know the phrase "for she loved much" refers to the evidence that she was already forgiven is because Jesus said, your sins "have been" forgiven (v. 48). This is the perfect tense, which shows the action as completed in the past with the results continuing into the present. When Jesus spoke these words, He was not then forgiving her; he was reaffirming and reassuring her. "Your sins have been forgiven . . . and are still forgiven."

Just as love received leads to love given, grace received leads to grace given. Now let's look at the Macedonians' grace.

2 Corinthians 8.1: "Now, brethren, we wish to make known to you the grace of God which has been given in the churches of Macedonia."

Have you ever heard someone sanctimoniously say, "It's not the money; it's the principle of the thing." We all know that likely it really is the money. In 2 Corinthians 8–9, it's not the money—it really is the principle. Money is not even mentioned except euphemistically. Instead, Paul uses descriptive words and phrases applying them to the gift and the giver: grace (v. 1), abundance of joy (v. 2), wealth of their liberality (v. 2), favor (lit., grace) of participation/fellowship (v. 4), support/service (v. 4), first gave themselves (v. 5), gracious (lit., grace) work (vv. 6,7); earnestness of others (v. 8); sincerity of your love (v. 8). The real subject is the powerful motivation of grace. Being filled with grace, not filling the church coffers, is the Holy Spirit's emphasis.

2 Corinthians records the fiscal sacrifice being given by the Macedonians to the needy saints in Jerusalem. It is a living sacrifice of the gospel-heart, grace-heart, new-heart that motivates it. Their giving grace is based upon the grace-giver. Our purpose is to see that grace is both the cause and the effect of giving grace to God's purposes and people's needs. But this chapter is about more than just giving money because grace is bigger than our pocketbooks. So don't limit the thought of giving to finances only. Think of giving whatever God has given to you, and especially the giving of you. That's the true gift of grace.

Grace, itself a gift, was given because the Macedonians gave. Grace, a practical gift, was given to help them give. Meditate on the following questions:

- Does it take grace to give?
- Do we receive grace by giving?

- How much of God's grace is working through us?
- How much of God's grace do we have?
- How many of God's gifts are we willing to receive?
- Are we willing to give God's grace to get God's grace?

Giving is serving others by sacrificing ourselves to God. Giving is receiving grace in order to give grace.

Hearing about others' good work is beneficial by being both uplifting and challenging unless we have closed our hearts. Paul ties the whole collection for needy saints to the gospel (v. 9), which includes words like grace (v. 1). Paul is a master motivator. He knows that a challenge perceived without commanding the challenge can work positively for good. But I want us to understand something right up front. In this text of Paul's, which is really the Holy Spirit's, we see some very adroit verbiage. Paul's selective vocabulary, though, is not self-serving. He is trying to help others do what they already know they should do and can do so that they can receive God's grace too.

Here at the very beginning of Paul's appeal, the real appeal is the grace of God.

> Right here, we have the full depth of Paul's view. All our fruit of good works, all our beneficence, and contributions of money are God's unmerited favor to us, his undeserved gift to us.... It is a treasure that he and his grace deposit in our basket. Blessed is he who has his basket overflowingly full of such gifts of God! Those who refuse to give, turn their basket away when God wants to place another gift into it. Ah, they keep their gift and lose the gift to themselves which their gift might have been. (Lenski, 1126–1127)

Simply put, if we keep our baskets full of what we have, we don't make room for what God has!

You have probably heard the illustration before, but it bears repeating. A Christian dies and goes to heaven. As he is being shown around, he notices warehouses of various sizes. Some large, some small. When he asks his angelic guide what they are, he is told he could investigate. He discovers his warehouse is a rather large one. His angelic guide informs him the warehouse contains all the blessings God had for him. As the new heavenly resident walks around, he does not recognize anything. "How can these be my blessings if I never received them?" The answer . . .? "You never asked!"

But beyond just asking, is simply being ready to serve. Christians are simply conduits for God's grace. Like a conduit, God uses us to transfer His blessings to others. By working through us, He is able to bless those needing His help. So, when thinking of being a con-du-it, think, I "can-do-it"!

2 Corinthians 8.2: "That in a great ordeal of affliction their abundance of joy and their deep poverty overflowed in the wealth of their liberality."
The Macedonians had two overwhelming problems that did not overwhelm them. These two problems were persecution (or some kind of affliction) and poverty (possibly due to harsh treatments from the Romans and previous civil wars prior to dominion by Augustus). Let's examine these words and concepts, for there is a wealth of learning in this verse. Their persecution is a great "ordeal":

> As the metal of coins was tested as to its genuineness, so the Macedonians have just undergone a severe "test of affliction" (genitive of cause). (Lenski, 1127)

Have you ever noticed that troubles introduce us to ourselves? Troubles bring out our best or our beast. The Macedonians' ordeal had two effects: joy and poverty. An odd couple, and what a contrast. It is a paradox, but then again, grace is a paradox. The essence and foundation of Christianity are embracing the paradoxical through thinking, believing (i.e., accepting), and living paradoxically. If we Christians are not growing properly in the grace of God, it is because we do not fully explore the paradoxical essence of Christianity found in thinking, believing (i.e., accepting), and living paradoxically. The Macedonians lived in grace and lived the paradoxes of Christianity.

What overflows is not the Macedonian's money, for they are in deep poverty. What overflows is their liberality and generosity. We can be a liberal giver without giving much; or a miserly giver while giving abundance. Do you remember the rich givers and the widow who gave two small copper coins (Mk. 12.41–44)? Who gave more?

Speaking of joy, have you ever noticed the similarity between miserly and misery? They both come from the same Latin word, miser, meaning wretched. Miserly people are miserable people. We see the exact opposite connection in our text. Our English word cheerful (9.7) comes from the Greek word hilaros—from which we get "hilarious." I am not saying that we have to laugh out loud when the collection basket comes by, but we should be cheerful. How can that be? Grace. In giving, we are being like God, the originator of grace. While it is impossible to describe and capture all of what God is in a single word, we could begin with "giver." Our God is a giver. Our God loves to give gifts. Our God is capable of giving gifts. Our God has gifts to give.

- John 3.16: "For God so loved the world, that He gave His only begotten Son, that whoever believes in Him shall not perish, but have eternal life."
- James 1.17: "Every good thing given and every perfect gift is from above, coming down from the Father of lights, with whom there is no variation or shifting shadow."
- Matthew 7.11: "If you then, being evil, know how to give good gifts to your children, how much more will your Father who is in heaven give what is good to those who ask Him!"

Again speaking of joy, do a little extra study in how Paul uses the word in 2 Corinthians (1.24; 2.3; 6.10; 7.4,7,9,13,16; 8.2). Some brethren look and act like they have been weaned on a dill pickle instead of the grace of God. Joy wasn't the Macedonians only experience. They experienced the depths of dearth. Poverty overflowing into wealth is an oxymoron. English is filled with oxymorons: sweet sorrow, good grief, congressional ethics committee, and so on. Apparently, grace creates oxymorons— "the wealthy poor," "the joyfully afflicted."

The Macedonians' wealth is not material, but spiritual generosity. The Macedonians' wealth is grace. Which statement describes the Macedonians?

- Spent more than they could afford
- Gave more than they could afford

Which statement describes us?

- Spend more than we can afford
- Give more than we can afford

Notice, both are "spending"—one on ourselves—and the other for God. Look at what the grace of God (v. 1) can accomplish:

- Even when persecuted, the Macedonians can have an abundance of joy
- Even when poor, they can overflow in their wealth of liberality

Those are gifts from God far grander than physical blessings because they are gifts of grace. However, God's grace can only be effective if we let Him into our hearts. Grace received is grace given.

2 Corinthians 8.3: "For I testify that according to their ability, and beyond their ability they gave of their own accord."

"They made a joy of robbing themselves" (Lenski, 1128). Again, what an odd couple, what an oxymoronic statement—they robbed themselves, giving beyond what they had to give. Being self-motivated instead of forced creates an atmosphere of volunteerism and joy. Of their own accord—literally "self-chosen"—shows their contribution was not commanded but volunteered. They did not have to be "guilted" into giving. Even today, giving is voluntary. They didn't ask, "Do we have to?"

One of the great ironies in charity is that often the poor are more generous than the rich. Due to their own need, they realize that what few blessings they possess actually come from God and therefore belong to God. When we possess little, we possess more than our possessions. Our needs awaken us to the needs of others. Having lived through many hurricanes in South Florida, neighbors were the most generous after a hurricane, when they often had been left with very little. Neighbors would share what little they had when everyone had little to give. They were grateful to be alive. Grace received is grace given.

Speaking of giving, at the bottom of our checks, we sign our names. Giving to the church or charity, we sign our names. By doing so, we are affirming two important facts. First, the money is in the bank. Second, the money is ours. The spiritual question is—is the money really ours? Or is it actually the grace of God which has been given to us?

A couple of parents sat around the dinner table with their family regaling their children with Christmas stories of how they would anonymously give needy people money. One year they had quietly approached the front door of a needy family, laid the money in an envelope, rang the doorbell, and ran. One year they spent far more on others than themselves. Probably the most enjoyable was when they would send money orders to friends in other cities inside a sealed, addressed envelope for them to mail. The recipients would be filled with joy and confusion— "Honey, do we know anyone in Chicago?" The joy was in giving, in giving anonymously, and knowing that such was a gift of grace. No names signed at the bottom, just prayers ascending up to heaven, and grace coming down.

The principle of the thing is about more than giving money. Living the Christian life is about living according to our ability and beyond our ability by the grace of God. Grace is how we live, survive, and thrive. Grace received is grace given.

2 Corinthians 8.4: "Begging us with much urging for the favor of participation in the support of the saints."

Standing on the side of the road in almost any city, there are beggars. Such a sad sight this is to see. Sitting in the pews in almost any church, there are not enough beggars. This, too, is a sad sight to behold. If what you just read did not shock you, go back and read it again—you missed what I wrote. Yes, we need more beggars in churches today. Not beggars to get, but beggars to give. The Macedonians were beggars, but they didn't beg for money; they didn't beg because they were "work challenged." They begged to serve. They begged to work. They begged to be involved in giving God's grace to others. They begged by their generosity to receive God's grace.

How often do we see this happen today? People begging to give more, do more, and consequently, be more? We see this same attitude in the early days of the nation of Israel when building the tabernacle (Ex. 35.20–36.7). Where does such a response come from? Grace! For the Israelites, they have just experienced God's grace in being released from slavery. Also, the Israelites have "plundered" the Egyptians and must have viewed everything they had as coming from God. The Macedonians likewise had an attitude of grace. They had the right attitude, heart, and the knowledge that everything they had already belonged to God: money, time, job, children, wife, and self (Matt. 10:34–39; Lk. 12.33–34).

A literal translation of v. 4 reads: "the grace (*charis*) and the fellowship (*koinonia*) of the service (*diakonia*) of the saints." Does that sound like something you would like to be part of? That sounds far more spiritual than the NASB translation— "the favor of participation in the support of the saints." Grace is about fellowship and service. Grace is about belonging and serving. Grace received is grace given.

2 Corinthians 8.5: "And this, not as we had expected, but they first gave themselves to the Lord and to us by the will of God."

Question: is it more difficult to give of yourself or to give of your money? We in America are generally greatly blessed materially; it is much easier to give money than ourselves. We can give a little and not even miss it. Giving money can be too easy for us. This is a constant danger, because if it is easy, then maybe we are doing it on our own and don't need God and His grace. Think about that, and then expand the giving from money to giving ourselves. Some have more money than time. Others have more time than money. Either can be used by God. The problem is when we have too much of ourselves and God has too little. "The crowning point of their generosity was their complete self-surrender." (Plummer, in Tasker, 113).

Because of the verse division in this text (and the way most translations punctuate it), I did not understand this verse. I used to think the phrase "and this, not as we had expected" described what followed—"but they first gave themselves to the Lord and to us by the will of God." But that is not the reference point. Isn't it expected that we first give of ourselves? Verses

3–5 are one long sentence in the NASB. What the apostle did not expect was the begging, ability, and generous amount, however small, given by the Macedonians. Paul knew they didn't have the resources. Therefore they surprised him. Grace allows for surprises. Grace produces surprises. Grace produces ability where there is disability. Paul then describes how this was done: "they first gave themselves to the Lord." This is also a mark of them receiving God's grace. If we want to receive God's grace, we have to first give ourselves to God.

Let's illustrate the right (and wrong) attitude with a parable I heard years ago that we'll call, The Parable of the Golden Quarter:

> In a congregation, there is a miserly [remember the connection between miserly and misery?] "Christian" who never gave anything, anytime, anywhere. Whenever the collection basket is being passed, all in the congregation know that when it comes to giving, he religiously observes the "passover." Therefore they would pass over him.
>
> One Sunday, a new Christian is passing the basket. This young Christian is unfamiliar with this "passover" observance and stands, holding the basket, right next to the miserly gentleman. Well, the gentleman goes into his routine of sticking his hand into his pocket and jiggling his change. Usually, the basket would ordinarily pass on by him. This new convert, though, is unfamiliar with this custom and continues to stand and wait. Jiggle . . . wait . . . jiggle . . . wait . . . jiggle . . . wait. The old man grows embarrassed, and the young man just patiently waits [don't you just love new converts!]. Finally, as the tension in the room rises, along with the temperature, the miserly Christian hastily reaches for a quarter in his pocket and gives it. The contribution continues as normal.
>
> Later, the old man goes home and takes all the change out of his pocket. Something is missing, and it isn't a quarter. He had accidentally given a $50.00 gold piece. Let me correct myself. The church received a $50.00 gold piece. The old man gave a quarter. Grace not received is grace not given.

The Corinthian Church

Before discussing the Corinthian Church, notice the words preceding this man-made chapter division: "I rejoice that in everything I have confidence in you" (7.16). Paul is a masterful persuader. Anyone who has a biblically sound and deep understanding of grace can be too. Notice the psychological "set-up":

- Step 1: Paul commends the Corinthians
- Step 2: Paul cites the grace-filled example of the Macedonians
- Step 3: Paul challenges the Corinthians

2 Corinthians 8.6: "So we urged Titus that as he had previously made a beginning, so he would also complete in you this gracious [lit., grace] work as well."

"The connecting words . . . imply that as a result of the Macedonians' generosity and total commitment of themselves to the Lord, Paul is encouraged to take steps to bring about the completion of the collection among the Corinthians." (Tasker, 113) In other words, the Macedonians were motivated by the grace-giver, and the Corinthians were to be motivated by grace receivers. Why should this motivate the Corinthians?

If God is able to complete the work in the Macedonians, He can complete it in the Corinthians.

If the Corinthians hear that others have not only begun a work but also finished it, they might feel _____ (plug in whatever emotion works best for you: encouraged, challenged, guilty, pressured, etc.) and therefore complete their task, also.

But notice in what Paul challenges them—in that which they had already challenged themselves. Prodding people to do what they have already purposed is much easier than getting people to do what we want. Paul never persuaded people for his own benefit, only for the welfare of others. How often do we Christians, with extremely good intentions, make promises to perform a certain task(s) and never finish it? Sadly, more often than not. I know I have been guilty of this. When we do this, we are not only neglecting our duty, we are missing God's grace.

Ask yourself and your church:

- What do we need to do?
- What do we need to promise?

- What have we already promised?
- What do we need to finish?

Now get busy and get grace!

2 Corinthians 8.7: "But just as you abound in everything, in faith and utterance and knowledge and in all earnestness and in the love we inspired in you, see that you abound in this gracious work [lit., grace] also."

As noted before, Paul is a master motivator—maybe a grace-inspired psychologist. Just read Philemon sometime. If we are told that we are so-gifted by God and that it would be good for us to receive another gift of God, wouldn't we want to? That's Paul's approach.

Notice again the emphasis on grace. The NASB says, "gracious work," but the literal translation is "grace." Was Paul motivating them to show grace, participate in grace, or receive grace? Whatever the answer, the answer is filled with grace.

Everything else mentioned in this verse the Corinthians already abounded in: faith, utterance, knowledge, earnestness, love—which are gifts from God. All of them are specifics of God's grace. Grace received is grace given.

2 Corinthians 8.8: "I am not speaking this as a command, but as proving through the earnestness of others the sincerity of your love also."

Nothing can help us see these contrasting attitudes any better than a few lighthearted illustrations.

1. A rookie cop, taking an examination, is asked what he would do to break up a crowd. "I'd take up a collection," he said.
2. The hat is passed around one Sunday morning in a penny-pinching church. The hat is returned absolutely empty. The preacher raises his eyes toward heaven and says reverently, "Oh Lord, I thank thee that at least I got my hat back."
3. A preacher is called by the Internal Revenue Service about a $2,500 contribution claimed by one of the members. "Did he really give that

amount?" the investigator asks. The preacher reflects a moment, then says, "I'd rather not say right now, but if you'll call back tomorrow, I am quite sure the answer will be yes."

Money and Christians . . . an uneasy relationship. A preacher from the past, Marshall Keeble, said:

> I've been told that you can't preach much on giving, that such preaching will kill a church. Well, you show me the church that ever died from giving too much, and I will climb up on top of that meeting house and lay down my woolie head on dem moss-covered shingles, and I will say, "Blessed Are The Dead Which Die In The Lord."

Is giving on Sunday an obligation? Is that what Paul teaches in 2 Corinthians? No. He is teaching that giving is a privilege we have volunteered to do. Giving allows us to experience the grace of God. How? It's not that we are buying the grace of God, but rather we are experiencing God because God, in grace, gave to us His Son.

When Christians ask regarding a spiritual activity, "Where does it say I have to," they are asking for a particular law. If they do not have the right heart, they will not obey the law even if shown that it is in the Bible. And if they do obey, it will be the letter of the law and not from a sense of grace. They do it grudgingly and under compulsion (2 Cor. 9.7). There is no sense of sharing in God's grace.

What would be the reaction of many Christians upon hearing that the contribution is voluntary and that they did not have to give? "Yahoo! Papa is getting a new motorcycle!" Or . . . "So, what's your point? I'd give anyway."

Which type of motivation do we respond to more readily and more completely?

> Paul is not issuing orders to the Corinthians as a commander who is simply to be obeyed; he is doing a far deeper thing, he is using the loving earnestness of others (the Macedonians) as a simple means for testing the genuineness of the love of the Corinthians. He is giving the Corinthians an opportunity to compare their love with the love the Macedonians manifested in their great earnestness. The

genuineness of what the Macedonians are showing is beyond question; it is, then, a good means for testing the Corinthians. (Lenski, 1135)

If others are doing good works which we excuse ourselves from doing, can we say we have the same sincerity as they? Can we say we are enjoying and receiving the grace of God as much as they? But don't allow me to "guilt" you into anything. Do allow me to "grace" you into everything.

2 Corinthians 8.9: "For you know the grace of our Lord Jesus Christ, that though He was rich, yet for your sake He became poor, that you through His poverty might become rich."

Please read that above verse again. There is "richness" in this verse, and depth far deeper than the few words used by the Holy Spirit. Describe for me Jesus' wealth that He gave up. Now describe for me the poverty He experienced. Do any of us feel adequate to such a task? This, my friend, is the motivation behind our motivation.

When I was a kid, I tried to grasp what Jesus gave up. The best that I could come up with is that God becoming a man would be comparable to man becoming an ant. I'd look down at the tiny speck of fragility and think . . . that's still not enough of a difference. Then I would squash the ant. (Hey, theological lessons for a kid can only last so long!) But wait, I can extend this theological analogy. Didn't Jesus become poor instead of squishing us like bugs, like we deserve? Didn't Jesus become poor and get stepped on by humanity Himself? Jesus became poor so that we could become rich.

As an adult, if I tried to intellectually grasp what Jesus did in not regarding equality with God a thing to be grasped (Phil. 2.6), I could delve into ontological essentiality and economical realities. Grant it, such a discussion would be fun and profitable, but ultimately inadequate in its totality. If I were to try to explain the mundane practicalities of Jesus' daily incarnation experiences, the result would seem ironically ordinary. If I stooped as He stooped and pictured how He suffered the banal indignities of being flesh, I fear such specific details would appear inappropriate. Use your imaginations. If I tried to grasp and describe the real poverty, I would still fail. If I were to compare His transformation of wealth to poverty to any human experience, ultimately, human wealth is not rich enough, and Jesus' poverty is far too poor. And yet, that is exactly what the Holy Spirit does through Paul. Inspiration uses the gospel, the example of Jesus, as the supreme example of giving, of living, of poverty, of wealth, and of grace. "Grace" is used both of Jesus' giving and the Macedonians' giving (v. 1). Both gave out of poverty; both gave of themselves (v. 5). Grace does not just save us; it motivates us to consider the needs of others above ourselves. It considers the spiritual relationship more essential than our physical realities. When giving of ourselves first (8. 5), we are living the Gospel—we are imitating Jesus' giving of Himself. How's that for motivation?

Do we see what He gave? How does Jesus' giving compare with what we give? Got you to stutter there, didn't I? It doesn't even begin to compare—if we are comparing His life to our money. However, in a small way, we can make a comparison that we can relate to ourselves. Jesus, the Philippians, and the Macedonians all gave of themselves—so have this attitude in yourselves (Phil. 2.5). All gave of themselves to give grace. Are we? That's living the gospel. That's living grace. That's living.

Giving of ourselves is a sacrifice. Let me take a minute and ask a question. How do you define "sacrifice?" Is it something that we simply "give up?" Is a sacrifice defined by our losing something? "Yeah, I sacrificed my time at work to be at church today." And then we sigh a holy sigh. I would like to challenge that thinking; I believe that not only is it fundamentally flawed, but it creates a negative attitude.

Baseball can teach us a theological lesson here. What is a sacrifice bunt? It is when a batter bunts the ball, knowing that he, the batter, will be thrown out, but bunts nevertheless in order to advance a runner on the bases. What is a sacrifice fly? It is a long fly ball that is caught for an out, but it is hit deep enough in the outfield that a runner can tag the base he is on and advance. In both instances, when the batter "sacrifices" his "at bat," he helps the team. He gives to the team. And the team gives him a high five.

The International Standard Bible Encyclopedia gives a summary definition of sacrifice: "Sacrifice is thus a complex and comprehensive term. In its simplest form, it may be defined as 'a gift to God'" (e-sword). The English word "sacrifice" is related to "sacred." A sacrifice is not us giving up something; it is us giving to Someone—God. Does that put a different spin on offering a sacrifice? Jesus did not simply give up His life, He gave to us and His Father. We give to others and to God. To give a sacrifice is to give and receive grace.

2 Corinthians 8.10: "I give my opinion in this matter, for this is to your advantage, who were the first to begin a year ago not only to do this, but also to desire to do it."

In giving his opinion, Paul is concerned about the Corinthian's welfare and the well-being of the saints, not his own welfare. All of us would learn a valuable lesson by only giving our opinion when it is to the other's advantage. Have you ever known someone that believed everyone else had a right to his opinion? "Opinionizing" only when it helps others could be our grace-gift to others and ourselves.

But notice the "psychological goading." "You were first, to desire. You were before the Macedonians. You did well." Willingness and desire do not always equate to performance and completion. Sometimes we need living examples and reminders. So Paul gives them the Macedonians. Can you think of someone who could encourage you?

2 Corinthians 8.11: "But now finish doing it also; so that just as there was the readiness to desire it, so there may be also the completion of it by your ability."

How often do we desire a work (or anything), and the desire that started it does not finish it? Many Christian lives are the same. I don't know about you, but I am a whole lot better at beginning things than finishing them. How many "church programs," get started with a bang, only to end with a thud? Now let's make this personal . . . how many of us have started diets, tried to quit smoking, began our yearly read-through-the-Bible plan, and failed? As someone said, "Quitting smoking is easy, I've done it a thousand times!" We get the point.

Review your life and remember what you wanted to accomplish. Sometimes plans can be unrealistic, and that is why we quit. The goal of the Corinthians was within their grasp. The reality of the goal wasn't their problem. The reality of the giver was. Sometimes plans fail because of the planner — you and me.

2 Corinthians 8.12: "For if the readiness is present, it is acceptable according to what a person has, not according to what he does not have."

I hope that none of you thought I was soliciting people to give what they cannot afford to give—even if the Macedonians did . . . even if the widow did. No one has the right to ask anyone to give according to what they do not have. Preachers receiving signed-over Social Security checks are a dis-"grace," dishonor, humiliation, and embarrassment to Christianity.

2 Corinthians 8.13: "For this is not for the ease of others and for your affliction, but by way of equality."

There is an old saying, "Give till it hurts." Wrong. God wants us to give until it feels good.

2 Corinthians 8.14: "At this present time your abundance being a supply for their need, so that their abundance also may become a supply for your need, that there might be equality."

What does this verse mean? What did the Corinthians have an abundance of? The answer is either material or spiritual, either material wealth or spiritual wealth. Either they had an abundance of money, or they had an abundance of grace. Or possibly they had an abundance of opportunity.

What did the recipients have an abundance of? Poverty and opportunity to receive. How does a need in Jerusalem become a supply for the Corinthians? The answer is equality, balance, and understanding of why God blesses us. The answer is an opportunity to reenact the gospel on some small level. God blesses us with grace and material goods so that we can help others. If God does not bless us with prosperity, He is blessing us with the opportunity to be the recipients of grace from others . . . or to reach down in the depths of our poverty and help others anyway. Either way, God is giving grace.

We can see this equality in the next verse, where we learn that all have what is necessary.

2 Corinthians 8.15: "As it is written, "He who gathered much did not have too much, and "he who gathered little had no lack."

Paul gives a different definition to equality. It is not mathematically equal in material things, but equal in having what is needed (not wanted). This applies in the overall, general life-style of the Christian and the church. Each of us has gifts of grace (1 Pet. 4.10). Some have more than others, therefore more responsibility. But that does not mean the lesser gifted should always be receiving and never giving. We all have gifts given to us by God, and we should be sharing them.

The Old and New Testaments contain examples of people who had the wrong ideas about wealth. They considered material blessings a sign of their righteousness. Maybe instead, material blessings should be considered a sign of how righteous God wants us to be—how righteously we can share—even if the righteous giving exceeds the righteous gift.

Let's skip down to our conclusion, chapter 9, starting with verse six:

2 Corinthians 9.6-11: "Now this I say, he who sows sparingly will also reap sparingly, and he who sows bountifully will also reap bountifully. Each one must do just as he has purposed in his heart, not grudgingly or under compulsion, for God loves a cheerful giver. And God is able to make all grace abound to you, so that always having all sufficiency in everything, you may have an abundance for every good deed; as it is written, "He scattered abroad, he gave to the poor, his righteousness endures forever." Now He who supplies seed to the sower and bread for food will supply and multiply your seed for sowing and increase the harvest of your righteousness; you will be enriched in everything for all liberality, which through us is producing thanksgiving to God."

Please take caution in understanding what is meant here. Too many preachers use 2 Corinthians 9 to motivate people to give a lot of money to them and their causes. Their motivation technique is not grace, but greed—greed on their part and on the part of the contributors. "Give me your money," they say, "and God will give you more money in return!" These people should anger and sadden us (Mk. 3.5). Preachers of that ilk are encouraging people to exchange God's grace for mere coinage. That is just as bad as those ungodly persons who turn the grace of our God into licentiousness (Jude 1.4).

Modern history has shown that too many preachers know more about money than the grace of God. If that sounds harsh, I meant it to be. This is how too many interpret this section: "he who sows sparingly financially shall also reap sparingly financially, and he who sows bountifully financially shall also reap bountifully financially." They make the motivation for giving, receiving more money in return. They make God a divine interest-bearing CD. Or worse, a slot machine! They preach a "health and wealth gospel." They tell you to give to God and then give you their address! I would like to point out that none of the money Paul received from the Macedonians and Corinthians for the saints in Jerusalem went to him. He didn't even charge a "shipping and handling fee."

That which is sowed is good deeds (v. 8). But notice what the Corinthians reaped—"God is able to make all grace abound to you" (v. 8). The Holy Spirit did not promise a 100 percent increase on our contributions. He promises us grace. Which would we prefer? If God promised us either one million dollars or enough grace to give one million dollars, which would we choose? I'll ask again, which would we prefer?

Consider the selfishness that some say God is catering to. And then consider the selflessness that God is truly promising.

2 Corinthians 9.12–14: "For the ministry of this service is not only fully supplying the needs of the saints, but is also overflowing through many thanksgivings to God. Because of the proof given by this ministry, they will glorify God for your obedience to your confession of the gospel of Christ and for the liberality of your contribution to them and to all, while they also, by prayer on your behalf, yearn for you because of the surpassing grace of God in you."

Thanksgivings, glorifications, confession of the gospel, and surpassing grace—all because the saints had enough grace to give.

> The ground on which the saints at Jerusalem would praise God was the manifestation of the Christian fellowship, which the Corinthians cherished not only for them but for all believers. It was the consciousness of the communion of saints—the assurance that believers, however separated, or however distinguished as Jews and Gentiles, bond or free, are one body in Christ, that called forth their praise to God. And, therefore, the apostle says it was the (koinonia) fellowship of the Corinthians not only towards them, (the saints in Jerusalem,) but towards all believers, that was the ground of their praise. (Charles Hodge, 226)

In other words, God gives us grace to give, which enables us to give grace to others, resulting in grace being given even beyond understanding.

2 Corinthians 9.15: "Thanks be to God for His indescribable gift!"

After studying this text, what do you think that indescribable gift is? It is grace! This is the grace that the Macedonians experienced that enabled them to receive grace to give grace. This is the forgiveness the woman received, creating a love given back to the grace-giver at the Pharisee's house. This is the grace the Corinthians needed to remember. This is the grace, which is the gospel of Jesus Christ, who became poor so that He could give riches. This is the grace that does not ask, "Do I have to?" Give yourself and get grace. Grace received is grace given. How's that for motivation?

Questions

1. In Luke 7.36–50, how did grace motivate the woman to do what she did? Did her great love lead to her forgiveness or did her forgiveness lead her to great love?

2. In Luke 7, how does the parable of the two debtors illuminate the motivation of the woman?

3. From 2 Cor. 8, what verses show the result of grace and how it motivated the Macedonian church?

4. Using the Macedonians as an example, what can we learn about grace motivating giving monetarily and of ourselves?

5. How can grace motivate us to be a conduit of grace?

6. Using 2 Cor. 8, how do we see that grace received resulted in grace given?

7. For what did the grace filled but afflicted and poverty-stricken Macedonians beg for?

8. What can we learn from the Macedonians begging?

_____

_____

9. Which is more difficult, to give of ourselves or of our money?

_____

_____

10. From 2 Cor. 8 – 9, what does generosity give to the giver?

_____

_____

11. From 2 Cor. 8.9, how can what Jesus gave up motivate our generosity of giving?

_____

_____

_____

12. What lessons can we learn from 2 Cor. 8 – 9 regarding the desire to do something good and the importance of the completion of doing it?

_____

_____

13. From 2 Cor. 8.14 – 15 teach what principle?

_____

14. Does our lack of gifts, whether monetarily or in some talent negate our giving if we are motivated by grace?

15. How can many preachers use 2 Cor. 9 with error and teach wrong motivation?

16. In 2 Cor. 9.11-14, what will the Corinthians' generosity produce?

17. What is the "indescribable gift" mentioned in 2 Cor. 9.15?

6

The Grace That Rekindles

2 Timothy 1.1–2.13

Picture this: while walking down a street, a hooded stranger corners you and pulls out a gun demanding your money or your life. What do you do? Give him your money, of course. Now let's change the scenario so that the gun being pulled out is only a toy gun. It is not real. What do you do? Would you still give him all your money? If you did, it wasn't because you were afraid of the gun.

Grace and a toy gun? Stay with me, because we are going to learn how death is a toy gun and how the subject of grace helps to keep our inner, spiritual fire burning bright for Jesus. Speaking of fire, let's move on to another analogy!

A large family had gathered at the old farmhouse for a reunion. Long after supper, the celebration moved indoors. Only the father of the clan ventured out to wander the vast acres in the dark. On his walk, the old man fell into a ditch and found himself sitting waist-deep in slimy mud, which, while being very uncomfortable, posed no immediate danger. Without moving he shouted, "Fire! Fire!"

Since fire is one of the most dreaded rural disasters, the celebrating family poured out into the night, frantic with fear. Upon finding the mired old man, one of his sons said, "Pa, you scared us to death. Why on earth did you yell 'Fire'?"

"Well, now," replied the patriarch, "if I'd 'a yelled 'Mud!' I'd 'a been here till spring plantin'" (source unknown).

Fire is a very powerful tool, weapon, and metaphor, both for good and evil. Ahh, the smell of lit matches; I love it! I am a potential pyromaniac. Legally, I have little opportunity to quench this thirst for starting fires. Starting my grill is acceptable, and yet, I have "accidentally" allowed too much gas to build up and then threw in a match! Bbbwwwuuussshhh goes the flame—which is pretty cool . . . or should I say, hot! But, walking around with no eyebrows is not a good look so . . . DON'T TRY THIS AT HOME!

While growing up in Virginia, my mother noticed my delight in starting fires. She controlled and guided this fun by letting me start the fires in our fireplace during the winter. I was good at it, too. When trying to build a good fire, use stout, dry wood, but begin with kindling. It is also imperative to keep stoking the bands of fire and adding more kindling to keep it going, which brings us to our application concerning something that is true with our spiritual fires also (hence, the metaphor of grace and fire). So, do try this in your soul.

The Grace that Rekindles

Let's ask two questions:

- Are we as spiritually strong as we could be?
- Are we as spiritually strong as we want to be?

Those are two very different questions. The first answer is obviously "no," but the second answer is not so clear. Let me illustrate. I have always considered myself an Arnold Schwarzenegger look-alike—that is, the Arnold Schwarzenegger "before" picture . . . before he had any muscles! So, am I as strong physically as I can be? No. Am I as strong physically as I want to be? No . . . and yes. I would love to have muscles. However, I would love to have muscles only if I don't have to lift any weights, exercise, or do anything strenuous. I want the gain, but not the pain. So, in reality, I am as strong as I want to be physically, simply because I am not willing to do what is necessary to become stronger.

Now, apply that same thinking to the question, "Are we as spiritually strong as we want to be?" If each of us is honest, the likely answer is a sad and dangerous "yes." We can change. But, only if we want to, and it might require some pain as our spirits strengthen.

When it comes to God's grace, we know it is needed when we have not been spiritually strong and therefore are in need of God's forgiveness. But is that all grace is good for? Is it only when I sin I need grace? There is more to God's grace than that one aspect. We also need God's grace to help us make better choices so we do not sin in the first place. God's grace can help us stay strong. So the question is, "Do we know how to use God's grace to stay strong?"

That is what this chapter is about—the grace of God that rekindles our gifts, our faith, our souls, ourselves. That is what 2 Timothy 1.1–2.13 is all about.

Rekindling ourselves is a very sad topic and yet extremely exciting. I do not know whether to describe it as sadly exciting or excitingly sad. Either way, it is oxymoronic, as is jumbo shrimp, thunderous silence, short sermon, military intelligence.

- It is sad because it shows the reality of losing our inner, spiritual fire for God.
- It is exciting because it also shows the way to kindle afresh that fire making it roar again.

Rekindling ourselves is an imperative topic because it shows how to keep our spiritual selves on fire for God. As long as there are Christians, there will always be Christians who need their inner fires to be rekindled:

- An immediate need: grace persuades me to stay strong
- A future need: grace prepares me for trials
- A constant need: grace prevents me from becoming complacent

Who does this lesson of God's grace rekindling faith apply to? There are three ways to look at it:

Everyone. All of us are either consciously or unconsciously cooling our inner fires. All of us need to rekindle it to face certain tests. Each of us is in constant need of refueling it—unless we have never kindled it in the first place.

The Offended. If you are offended that someone might suggest your fire needs to be rekindled, then your conscience has apparently been pricked. And as the old country proverb rightly observes, "The hit dawg howls the loudest."

The Unoffended. There are two types of unoffended people. Those so proud nothing inflames them, and those so humble everything involves them.

After reading and rereading Paul's second letter to Timothy, I do not believe Paul's protégé had let his inner spiritual fire die out or necessarily even die down. Instead, I believe Paul is inviting, even imploring, Timothy to stoke his strong inner fire even more because of Timothy's task ahead: namely, visiting the imprisoned Paul in Rome. What could happen to Timothy because of his visit? Would he become spiritually discouraged by seeing his mentor suffering? Would he also be imprisoned? After all, Paul is imprisoned for Christ. Would he, like Paul was sure to do, lose his life? Timothy had to be fully aware that death was the likely outcome for Paul at the end of his imprisonment. Was Timothy spiritually and emotionally prepared to live with Paul physically losing his life? In Paul's second letter, he is preparing Timothy, and maybe even himself, for the ordeal to come. Here, therefore, we learn another valuable lesson on how to keep ourselves on fire for God—we need to stoke the fire in others.

For whatever reason, Timothy needed his fire stoked. Nero had imprisoned Paul—the same Nero who, in his reign of terror, would cover Christians with tar and use them as candles for parties. Paul needed to prepare Timothy's inward fire in case there was an outward fire.

2 Timothy 1.1: "Paul, an apostle of Christ Jesus by the will of God, according to the promise of life in Christ Jesus."

Why does Paul say he is an apostle? Didn't Timothy already know that? Of course he did. Therefore, Paul's pointing it out for a purpose. Notice that he gives two reasons, the second of which will spread like wildfire throughout his text. The first is the will of God. Let me add one cautionary thought. Paul, by mentioning his apostleship, is not trying to pull rank on Timothy. If anything, it is Paul's way of showing Timothy that we should accept, for good or bad, God's plan and purpose for us. And for that, both Paul and Timothy needed God's grace. The second reason is connected to the promise of life. There is a reason why Paul mentions the promise of life in his introduction. He only does that twice, here and in his letter to Titus (1.2). Later, we will see the text reveal more to us concerning this. But until then, look for hints along the way as to why.

2 Timothy 1.2: "To Timothy, my beloved son: Grace, mercy, and peace from God the Father and Christ Jesus our Lord."

Beginning a letter with "grace" was common in the first-century. Today we might begin with "Hey, how are you? Hope all is well." Paul begins this short letter mentioning grace in his salutation (1.2) and concludes with the same word (4.22). In the first (1.9) and second (2.1) chapters, he again uses the term grace with application to our walk with God. To Paul, grace is much more than a salutation and a conclusion. We can see this because it permeates his writings, his life, and his thoughts. No, that is not strong enough. Grace is his life and his thoughts.

When reading this, remember that Paul is not simply writing a formula for using grace. Paul is writing to a friend, a "son" he has mentored. Older Christians need to take younger ones under their wings for instruction and strength (Titus 2), but also as examples of grace. Being kindled by grace makes this attitude and relationship happen. The bond of a grace-strengthened relationship knows no limits.

Because of being filled with grace, younger Christians need to, and can, respect the wisdom that should come with age. Again, being on fire from God's grace can light the fire of respect from others living in that same grace. It is sad indeed to witness a belligerent youth, and even sadder, to witness a foolish, older Christian. Neither will have the strength from grace (2.1), to deal with life's fires.

2 Timothy 1.3: "I thank God, whom I serve with a clear conscience the

way my forefathers did, as I constantly remember you in my prayers night and day."

Grace keeps a clear conscience because it relies on God. That did not change with the change in covenants.

Question: who do you want thinking about and praying for you? One of the greatest privileges and challenges is to pray for people by name. Why a privilege? Because God might use us to help save and strengthen someone's inner fire and, therefore, their immortal soul. Why a challenge? In order to pray for people, we need to know them. Getting to know people is getting harder and harder as we become a more closed society through fear and busyness. Having a greater understanding of our shared, internal grace experience is more powerful than any secular external force. Having shared in the grace of Jesus encourages us to pray for others. After all, isn't God giving grace all about God thinking of us? So, the people we want thinking about and praying for us are those whose kindled grace-fed fires are obvious to all. Paul's communication to Timothy that he was keeping him in his prayers night and day had to strengthen Timothy, as Paul was a great example of a grace-led life.

2 Timothy 1.4: "Longing to see you, even as I recall your tears, so that I may be filled with joy."

Ponder the phrase, "longing to see you." Paul is getting ready to die, and he knows it (4.6–8). Does Timothy? Tears fell once; they will fall again. Death, whether by natural means or through persecution, is coming.

Have you ever visited someone in the hospital for the last time? Have you ever walked into a room knowing they would never walk out? Have you ever sat by someone's bed watching their labored breathing, and then listening for the disquieting quiet breathing that followed? Now ratchet up the emotions and imagine visiting someone on death row—someone innocent on death row—who is on death row because of you. "What?" you might be thinking? "How was Paul on death row because of Timothy? Why was Paul on death row?" Answer: for preaching grace to hundreds and thousands of people . . . people like Timothy.

Now switch positions. You are the one in the hospital; you are the one on death row; you are the one longing to see your friend, family member, or loved one before you die. What would make all this easier? God's grace.

Like I said, Paul is getting ready to die, and he knows it (4.6–8). Does Timothy? After all, Paul had been released from his previous Roman imprisonment; surely God won't let him die! But this time, instead of being temporarily released from a Roman imprisonment to live for Christ, God will release Paul from a Roman imprisonment permanently to die for gain (Phil.1.21). And yet, it is still correct that God will not let Paul die even physically because of the resurrection (John 11.25–26). Death might come, but death will not stay. Paul had already been deserted by many (1.15) who had let their fire die. Paul was lonely for Timothy's spiritual fellowship. Again . . . grace! God's gift of grace comes in many forms; one form is that of friends who are experiencing the same grace.

Paul loves Timothy and is unashamed in that love and its acknowledgment. That love is also reciprocated from Timothy. What could cause such an attachment? What could cause a man who had no children to love another man as his own child? Grace. We are granted an internal look at this love by Paul's recorded remembrance of Timothy's tears. I have little doubt that the tears, like the love, were also reciprocated by Paul (Acts 20.19,37).

Men need to be unashamed to cry and express their love, especially concerning spiritual matters and with grace-sharers. "Grace Incarnate" wept (John 11.35). Relationships are important not only in keeping our fires of friendship burning, but also in using our friendship altruistically for another's spiritual benefit. If we are friends, both socially and spiritually, then encouragement and admonishment are all the more effective. When was the last time we saw a grown man cry? When was the last time we grown men cried? It is important to understand that Paul and Timothy's great and deep friendship was built upon them both being recipients of God's grace. Spiritual friendship is an instrument and a result of grace.

2 Timothy1.5: "For I am mindful of the sincere faith within you, which first dwelt in your grandmother Lois and your mother Eunice, and I am sure that it is in you as well."

Why does Paul mention twice, and so close together, Timothy's sincere faith being "within" or "in" him? Things like that make me go, hmmm. I find language incredibly interesting. Paul, being guided by the Holy Spirit, uses language very carefully. It is important to see Paul's handling of Timothy during this trying time. Through two remarkable women, Timothy was a living legacy of faith and grace. When Paul says, "I am sure," that is the same in Greek as "I am convinced" (v. 12). Trying times require confidence. And don't we all need to know someone believes in us?

Since I believe Paul is mentally, emotionally, and spiritually preparing Timothy for a personally trying work, we can learn from Paul a great motivating method—remind people of their faith. Do we all remember the strength and the fire of our faith when we decided to accept God's grace? Maybe we need someone to remind us.

Timothy's grandmother and mother were good examples of grace living, which is faithful living. Sometimes we need to hear about others—that they are believers in the same things we are—in order to stay strong. Yes, misery loves company, but so does everyone else.

Family can powerfully influence us for either God or Satan. Have you ever noticed the influence unbelieving family has on Christians when visiting from out of town? Either we become more faithful or less. There are three choices. We can leave them at home if they refuse to come with us. We can bring them with us if they accept our invitation. Or we can stay home with them. One of Paul's themes is that remembering God's grace helps us to be unashamed. Maybe that is why some miss services when friends or family are around. Are we ashamed to leave our friends to be with God's friends? Are we ashamed to leave our family to be with . . . our family? If we are, then we are not on fire with God's grace.

Just like fire, family can be both helpful and hurtful. Parents, we need to talk to our children about grace. If we are good parents, we will teach our children why we do what we do religiously or spiritually. We will teach them what the Lord says; we will teach them why "book, chapter, and verse" is important, and we will teach them why we respect God and His word. It is more than a legalistic, "thus saith the Lord!" It is that, and more, much more. It is grace!

To illustrate, let's take a quick detour. Grace is a wonderful tool to use in raising children. My wife and I often speak to our children about our giving them grace. When they disobey, they receive a consequence. Let's say the punishment is no TV. Every Friday night is family night in the Hall house. If one of our children is on restriction, it is lifted for family night. Why? Grace. We give them grace for family night because we do not want the punishment to include missing out on being with the family. The reason we show grace to our children and speak of it as "giving grace" is so that grace will become a real, tangible experience to them; that way, they can better understand God's grace. I'll tell you one thing, my kids love receiving their parent's gift of grace. We, in turn, hope this makes them appreciate God's greater grace.

So, you can see from this illustration that the family can exemplify God's grace. Be aware of the influence that demonstrating your grace-fired life can have on your family and look for rekindling or stoking your fires from your family members whose fires are burning brightly. Just as Paul reminding Timothy of his grandmother's and mother's faith was meant to encourage him, so may our relationships in our family encourage us, and we, in turn, encourage them.

2 Timothy 1.6: "For this reason I remind you to kindle afresh the gift of God which is in you through the laying on of my hands."

Paul will repeat, "For this reason" later (1.12, 2.10), and it's important that we see the connection. Whether or not Timothy is growing cool in his faith, Paul has confidence in him because of the past faith he has shown. This can stoke our inner fire by remembering, "Yes, I once had the strength I long for today. Yes, I remember responding to the love found in God's grace."

A man named Greg used to start meetings at his home by asking people, "When in your life did you feel closest to God?" What an awesome question! I'll ask it right now when in your life did you feel closest to God?

I'll wait for your answer. Still waiting. You did stop reading and started thinking, didn't you? Come on now, don't just skip over this and go to the next paragraph. It is too important a question to skip over. I'll wait . . . done? Good.

When in your life did you feel closest to God? The irony is that most likely it was not at a time when life was easy.

Consider that word picture: "kindle afresh." This word "denotes to kindle afresh, or keep in full flame (*ana*, up, or again, *zōos*, alive, *pur*, fire), and is used metaphorically in 2 Tim.1:6, where 'the gift of God' is regarded as a fire capable of dying out through neglect. The verb was in common use in the vernacular of the time" (Vine, 1098). Another definition describes it, "to kindle anew, rekindle, resuscitate" (Thayer, 37) Let's think about the word resuscitate. That is an important theme in this chapter, isn't it? Picture Paul saying, "I am about to die, you need to resuscitate your faith, Timothy." Remember that concept and connect it to God's grace.

To kindle afresh is a lively word picture. It has been used of a horse roused to his utmost (Thayer, 37). Have you ever been on such a horse? When I was around 12 years old, my family went to a dude ranch. I rode a smallish horse named Penny, after her copper-coat color. Some 35 years later, I still remember that horse's name. I can still see her in my mind. That should tell you something! One day we started on our walking trail . . . please notice it is called a "walking trail." My horse noticed that no one, and no horse, trailed behind. Without warning, and without asking my permission—as I would have voted "neigh"—Penny turned around. Then she ran very fast, and as I had let go of the reins, I held on for dear life to the saddle horn. She finally stopped when she came to her post. I shook. I guess we could say that she was roused to her utmost and was rekindled. As for me, I needed to be resuscitated!

Is Timothy's inner spiritual fire in danger of dying out? I don't think so, but it really doesn't matter because the process is the same for the strong and the weak. Isn't it ironic and humbling that those whose fire is robust need to follow the same process of rekindling as those whose fire is dying out? It's ironic because the strong are no different from the weak in what is needed. It's humbling because we forever need God. And we forever need reminding of His grace.

Timothy needs to rekindle the gift of God within him. Paul wants it hotter—Timothy will need it hotter. What is the gift? Although I have an idea (the gift of preaching the message of grace), the specific gift itself is not as important as the experience by Timothy through Paul's admonition to rekindle it. We Christians often need rekindling. From a practical point of view, it is impossible to separate our faith, our gifts, and God's grace. Our faith needs to be fired up so that we can use our gifts of God. People get depressed, emotionally downtrodden, and often feel spiritually weak. For our purposes, it doesn't matter what needs rekindling, because no matter what the gift is, grace is involved in expressing it. We all have gifts, and we need God's grace. And ultimately what is rekindled is not just the gift, but the person.

2 Timothy 1.7: "For God has not given us a spirit of timidity, but of power and love and discipline."

"Fear not," "don't be afraid," and similar calming words are the most frequent command in the Bible. Paul's words to Timothy are not comforting, but challenging. A spirit of timidity is a spirit of fear. Timidity (*deilias*) "signifies a fear that results from lack of faith (Matt.8:26; Mark 4:40). Compare 'the cowardly' (*deilos*) and 'the faithless' in Revelation 21:8" (Spain,114).

Fear is one of the most powerful of deterrents. Listen to the following with your heart:

> When I reflect deeply on my life and what I really want, it is not to be afraid. When I am afraid, I am miserable. I play it safe. I restrict myself. I hide the talent of me in the ground. I am not deeply alive—the depths of me are not being expressed. When I am afraid, a tiny part of me holds captive most of me, which rebels against the tyranny of the minority. When I am afraid, I am a house divided against itself. So more than anything else I want to be delivered from fear, for fear is alien to my own best interest or, to put it positively, I want to give myself generously, magnanimously, freely—out of love. I want to be able to take risks—to express myself, to welcome and embrace the future. I want to see what it is to be most deeply me. I want union with all of life and existence. I want to know and sense a oneness with others – with all humankind. I want to know warmth and closeness to give acceptance and understanding and support. I want to sacrifice myself freely, for this is when I am most alive, most me. I sense that the art of loving, the art of risk-taking, is my thing. (Gordon, in O'Connor, 136)

This sounds very similar to what Paul is encouraging and preparing Timothy to do.

Listen to a related thought:

> If you want to discover the difference which Jesus made to mankind, go to the New Testament to find out, the answer given is the casting out of people's lives of fear....It is fear which makes men selfish, it is fear which makes them hate, it is fear which make them blind, it is fear which makes them mad. Fear casts out love, as love casts out fear. Which of the two, therefore, am I going to choose? (Williams, in O'Connor, 136)

When looking at fear and animals, we can readily recognize four reactions. Strangely, we humans are not much different from animals in this respect, nor are we as Christians. Fear can produce four reactions, or more accurately, three reactions and one inaction.

Fear can paralyze us, which is inaction. Just think of the deer in the headlights.

Fear can cause us to run away. When God presents opportunities, and we don't take advantage of them, haven't we run away?

Fear can cause us to fight irrationally. Often, in trying to help hurting animals, they respond dangerously to their protector. But too many of us fight with one another. Why? We have the spirit of timidity and fear, instead of the spirit of grace.

Fear can cause us to fight righteously. We need to fight for our souls and for others. "It is a terrifying thing to fall into the hands of the living God" (Heb. 10.31).

Jesus spoke in terms of losing one's life in order to save it (Matt. 16.25). That kind of talk is not for timid souls, especially when the life we are losing is our tangible, breathing, fleshly life. Sometimes for Christ, we may have to lose our physical lives, but always we have to lose the selfish control of our lives. Most people would never willingly lose their life unless there is a cause or love greater than themselves. It is that love for Christ that should motivate us to let go of our fear and let Him control us instead of ourselves.

Because of fear, too many are hyper-cautious; they are always trying to minimize their risks to ridiculous extremes. Paul asks Timothy to remember his faith and the grace he received—a grace that cost Jesus his life, faith that is costing Paul his life, a rekindled faith that might cost Timothy his.

Forgetting our fear and remembering our faith requires power, love, and discipline. Instead of timidity and fear, God gives us power. Although this is the same Greek word translated "miracle," "Here, the power (is to) overcome all obstacles and to face all dangers. It is closely linked with the sense of . . . boldness." (Vincent, 290). This brings to mind one of my favorite verses: "Now to Him who is able to do far more abundantly beyond all that we ask or think, according to the power that works within us" (Eph. 3.20). Not fear, but power. Not fear, but love. Not fear, but discipline.

We cannot talk about grace without talking about love. As you probably expect, the love mentioned here is *agapē*—a love that seeks the best for the one being loved. Power . . . I like that. Love . . . I need that. But discipline? Why discipline? Because I need that more than I realize, especially when facing difficulties. I need to learn to control myself and my thinking. Fear is the lack of control. Notice the inter-relationship between the three:

- Power must be controlled or disciplined and motivated by love.
- Love is not weak but powerful and controlled or disciplined.
- Discipline without love of self, others, and God is self-abuse.

The power of discipline ironically is restraint:

> In verse 7, Paul points Timothy to the fact that he has the Spirit who gives us power, love, and discipline. By saying God has not given us a spirit of timidity, Paul shows how the Holy Spirit of God contrasts with the human spirit that grows timid in conflict. Power is that which the Spirit produces out of the fountain of life promised to us. Love is that which the Spirit produces that casts out all fear. Discipline is that which enables us to refrain from doing what legally we might have the right to do. (Barber, 12)

2 Timothy 1.8: "Therefore do not be ashamed of the testimony of our Lord or of me His prisoner, but join with me in suffering for the gospel according to the power of God."

Timidity leads to shame, "therefore do not be ashamed of the testimony of our Lord." Are we ever ashamed or embarrassed that we are Christians? If you quickly said to yourself, "No, never," you are a better Christian than I am. If you did answer, "No, never," consider that perhaps you are deceiving yourself out of shame or that your standard is not high enough.

Let's ask the same question somewhat differently, "Have any of us ever compromised our conscience and values because of others?" Is there anyone who has not? Even Peter did (Gal. 2). Why? We, whether or not we admit it, are sometimes ashamed of our Lord . . . or at least our relationship to the Lord. Can we all remember Peter's ironic denial that he would never deny the Lord (Matt. 26.33)? Can any of us forget that he actually denied Him three times (Matt.26.75)?

Shame for sin is a good thing. Shame of our Lord is not. Ashamed is the "feeling expressed by this word [that] has reference to incurring dishonor or shame in the eyes of men. It is the grief a man conceives from his own imperfections considered with relation to the world taking notice of them; grief upon the sense of disesteem. . . . Hence it does not spring out of a reverence for right in itself, but from fear of the knowledge and opinion of men" (Vincent, 342).

Since I believe that grace is a key aspect of our inner fire, how does grace help us become unashamed? "For both He who sanctifies and those who are sanctified are all from one Father; for which reason He is not ashamed to call them brethren" (Heb. 2.11).

How can I be ashamed of Jesus when He is not ashamed of me? If anyone deserves to be ashamed of anyone, it's the other way around. "For I am not ashamed of the gospel, for it is the power of God for salvation to everyone who believes, to the Jew first and also to the Greek" (Rom. 1.16).

How can I be ashamed of Jesus when He is my only hope? Shame on me for being ashamed of Jesus and His good news.

In essence, shame is a fear of consequences. With reference to our friends, we fear their ridicule, isolation, and other such temporal things. In 2 Timothy, the consequence is death. But death is that toy gun we began this chapter with and that we are slowly getting to understand.

If fear leads me to being ashamed of Jesus, how do we think we will treat those strong enough not to be ashamed of Him? More often than not we do not esteem those who are stronger than us when we are in denial of our own weakness and fear. Paul encouraged strength by asking, begging, and encouraging Timothy not to be ashamed of "me his prisoner." Have you ever had a friend who turned his back on you because of someone else? Have you ever been that friend? I have. I felt betrayed . . . and I have betrayed. The latter hurts more. I have turned on my friends and been turned on. I have disappointed loved ones and been disappointed. Jesus has likewise felt the sting of betrayal but never has He betrayed. More personally, never has He betrayed me. Paul had also felt the sting of betrayal (vv. 15–16). Can you hear the pain in the words, "Timothy, don't betray me!"?

As a further application, how can we be loyal to one another while gossiping, backbiting, and neglecting? Are we acting gracefully when committing those sins? The subject of grace can again help us to be loyal, not only to Jesus but to our fellow Christians.

2 Timothy 1.9: "Who has saved us and called us with a holy calling, not according to our works, but according to His own purpose and grace which was granted us in Christ Jesus from all eternity."

The theology of grace not only permeates Paul's thought, but his life. I have a purpose in life according to the eternal grace of God granted to me in Christ Jesus. Knowing this gives me strength to go on. Living according to my own purpose is the root of sin. Living for God's purpose is the foundation of grace. When afraid, we often lose sight of the obvious—our purpose and God's grace. Grace does not change our circumstances. It gives us the strength to handle life's situations. Circumstances do not need to change us if we are changed by grace. Too often, when we can't change the circumstances, the circumstances change us . . . negatively. Allowing our circumstances to positively change us can only happen if we stoke the fire within and fight fire with grace.

2 Timothy 1.10: "But now has been revealed by the appearing of our Savior Christ Jesus, who abolished death and brought life and immortality to light through the gospel."

Mentioning "life" is how Paul began his letter to Timothy (1.1). "Living in the shadow of death, Paul must have found much comfort in the good news that Jesus abolished death" (Spain, 116).

This is a key to understanding how grace rekindles our inner, spiritual fire. What need did Paul have to be afraid, thereby becoming ashamed of anything? Fear leads to shame; courage leads to glory. What need did Timothy have? What about us? This is essentially an argument from greater to lesser—if even losing my life does not matter, then nothing in life matters. That's how grace kindles our inner fire. I fear my mere words cannot capture the power of that thought.

Jesus gave the same assurance:

> Matthew 10.26–28: Therefore do not fear them, for there is nothing concealed that will not be revealed, or hidden that will not be known. What I tell you in the darkness, speak in the light; and what you hear whispered in your ear, proclaim upon the housetops. Do not fear those who kill the body but are unable to kill the soul; but rather fear Him who is able to destroy both soul and body in hell.

Death is not only an exit from life but an entrance to life, both spiritual and resurrected. Paul's, Timothy's, and our acceptance of God's grace is the key to opening that eternal door. This is where the toy gun and grace come together. Grace makes death as real as a toy gun. Why do we think the scriptures so often speak of death as being asleep? In a real sense, death is not real because it is not the end. A resurrection is coming! Our spirits are alive, and eternity is real.

Eternity and the resurrection are hallmarks of grace. Notice the doubt, fear, and timidity found in these otherwise great thinkers:

- Concerning a future life, Seneca said, "that which our wise men do promise, but they do not prove."
- Socrates, at his death, said, "I hope to go hence to good men, but of that I am not very confident; nor doth it become any wise man to be positive that so it will be. I must now die, and you shall live; but which of us is in the better state, the living or the dead, God only knows."
- Pliny said, "Neither soul nor body has any more sense after death, than before it was born."

- Cicero concluded after a discourse on the subject, "Which of these opinions is true, some god must tell us; which is most like to truth, is a great question." (Barnes, 215–216)

Now compare those to one who thrives from grace.

> 2 Timothy 4.6–8: For I am already being poured out as a drink offering, and the time of my departure has come. I have fought the good fight, I have finished the course, I have kept the faith; in the future there is laid up for me the crown of righteousness, which the Lord, the righteous Judge, will award to me on that day; and not only to me, but also to all who have loved His appearing.

I live even if I die. I live because I die. I live because Jesus lived, died, and lived again!

Let's get back to Paul's rekindling of Timothy . . .

2 Timothy 1.11: "For which I was appointed a preacher and an apostle and a teacher."

To me, this is the gift that Timothy needed to rekindle (v. 6). Timothy, like Paul, was appointed as a preacher and teacher. Our gifts from God are nothing without the faith and grace to use them. For an unbeliever, they are like a wrapped, unopened box sitting by itself. For a fearful believer, they are like an unwrapped, opened box sitting in the closet. They are useless. The gifts that God gives to us by His grace are also the gifts that are to be used because of God's grace. Paul said, "But by the grace of God I am what I am, and His grace toward me did not prove vain; but I labored even more than all of them, yet not I, but the grace of God with me" (1 Cor. 15.10).

Paul received God's grace to be saved and to be used; so did Timothy. Paul here is reminding Timothy to follow Paul's example, an example of grace by grace for grace. "Timothy," says Paul, "we are the same. Be like me."

2 Timothy 1.12: "For this reason I also suffer these things, but I am not ashamed; for I know whom I have believed and I am convinced that He is able to guard what I have entrusted to Him until that day."

Remember the last time Paul said, "For this reason" (v. 6)? Now he says, "Timothy . . . be like me as I am like Christ."

Follow Paul's line of self-assuredness:

- I suffer
- I am not ashamed
- I know
- I believe
- I am convinced
- I trust

Paul is assured about what is happening, why it is happening, how to react, and whom to trust. That, my friend, is another gift of grace. Problems, whether personal or professional, often produce doubt. When we know that our problems are not of our own doing caused by our sin, then our problems need not produce hesitancy, timidity, or uncertainty. Problems can produce a self-confidence that is not derived from the self but from grace.

Grace is not opposed to reason; grace produces reason and reasons. "For this reason" ties in with "the gift" (v. 6) in Timothy that needed to be rekindled. Timothy was a teacher. Paul, using himself as an example, was trying to encourage Timothy. Too often, when people use themselves as examples, their motivation is to make themselves look good, instead of helping others. Even if their motivation is properly aimed, other people consider it bragging and grandstanding. Both failures show a lack of grace within their own lives. The longer I am a believer, the more clearly I see that most problems within our lives are due to our bad relationship to God's grace.

"I know whom I have believed." What confidence! Paul's confidence is not based on man-generated faith, but on Christ: "I know whom I have believed" (2 Tim. 1.12). The word for "know" is *eidō*. It comes from a form of the word *horaō*. It means to know, to perceive. He knows something! He divinely understands something. The verb is in the perfect active tense, so his knowledge is because of something that has happened to him in the past. He has this clear perception.

What perception? "For I know whom I have believed . . ." Again, the perfect tense. *Pisteuo*, "believe" means to be so fully persuaded that one surrenders completely. Paul has many times in his past fully surrendered to Christ in any and all situations and Christ has never let him down. Paul's confidence is solidly based on his knowledge and experience of Christ. (Barber, 12)

Grace produces confidence. Grace produces results. Grace—knowing Jesus—can fan the flames within to face the flames without. Historically, those flames were real under the terror of Nero. One day they might be again.

This grace leads to confidence because we, like Paul, can say, "I am convinced that He is able."

> Verse 12 is like a tapestry, with each thought building on the others: "For this reason I also suffer these things, but I am not ashamed; for I know whom I have believed and I am convinced that He is able to guard what I have entrusted to Him until that day." Some translations say, "I am persuaded." The Greek word for "convinced," or "persuaded" is *peithō*, which appears also in v. 5 ("persuaded" or "I am sure"); and also in Romans 8.38: "For I am convinced that neither death, no life, nor angels, no principalities, nor things present, nor things to come, now powers" (Barber)

When you read that "God is able to guard what I have entrusted to Him," did your mind or tongue stumble over the words? This phrase actually struck me as strange. I expected it to read as "what He has entrusted to me." After all, hasn't Paul been emphasizing "the gift" and "grace?" But instead, he is confident and convinced that Jesus Christ is "able to guard what I have entrusted to Him until that day." What is it that we have entrusted to Him? Our immortal life, soul, and body!

God is able to guard/*phulassō* what believers trust Him to guard. To guard means to protect "against robbery or any loss." (Robertson, IV, 614). Paul confidently claims that he knows that whatever is being watched over will be kept perfectly protected. It is guarded by God. Death cannot rob me of life.

Grace-filled believers have entrusted our immortal lives, our souls, and our bodies to be resurrected to Jesus. We have "deposited" our faith in Him. Jesus

Christ is the best and safest bank in this world and the next (Matt. 6.19ff). Death does not rob us of life.

Notice the emphases:

- What I do: I believe; I am convinced; I have entrusted
- What does God do: He is able to guard

2 Timothy 1.13: "Retain the standard of sound words which you have heard from me, in the faith and love which are in Christ Jesus."

When we "retain," amazingly we are engaged in an action still connected to grace. We hold on to the words of grace—that Christ died for us, yes, but also that Christ conquered death for us. If we hold on to God's word, then we can keep ourselves rekindled inwardly. Plus, we can use the gifts God has given to us and rekindle others. We cannot change the message of grace. We cannot change any message from God. "Sound words" go beyond the death, burial, and resurrection of Christ. Sound words include our response to Jesus' grace-filled actions. Sound words involve our living in grace day by day. Retaining sound words is a humble submitting of ourselves to God, which is what grace is all about.

All this goes back to the gift (v. 6), which Timothy needed to rekindle, the same gift that Paul shares with him (v. 11). As Paul later states:

> 2 Timothy 4.2–5: Preach the word; be ready in season and out of season; reprove, rebuke, exhort, with great patience and instruction. For the time will come when they will not endure sound doctrine; but wanting to have their ears tickled, they will accumulate for themselves teachers in accordance to their own desires, and will turn away their ears from the truth and will turn aside to myths. But you, be sober in all things, endure hardship, do the work of an evangelist, fulfill your ministry.

2 Timothy 1.14: "Guard, through the Holy Spirit who dwells in us, the treasure which has been entrusted to you."

Wait a minute . . . living by grace is supposed to be easy, right? Then what do I have to guard? Why do I have to guard? The word "guard" is the same as is used of God in verse 12: God guards, and I guard. What is the treasure?

What has been entrusted to Timothy? Again, the word "entrust" is the same as the one found in verse 12: I have entrusted something to God, and God has entrusted something to me. How humbling, exciting, challenging, and frightening.

What is this treasure? Contextually it is related to grace, but grace is multifaceted. Is the treasure my salvation from sins? That is grace. Is the treasure my immortal life? That is grace. I am excited asking these questions because I am excited about the answer. Keep reading.

This isn't the first time Paul mentions this to Timothy. 1 Timothy 6.20: "O Timothy, guard what has been entrusted to you, avoiding worldly and empty chatter and the opposing arguments of what is falsely called knowledge."

What God has entrusted to Timothy, what Timothy needs to guard, is the same thing he needs to rekindle: namely, God's gift to Timothy and the message of that gift. Timothy is a preacher of the grace of God. Timothy is a preacher of immortal life. Timothy is a preacher of sound words. And Timothy needs to protect that message of grace and protect himself so as to stay true to that message. Others will manipulate God's grace (3.1–7). Some will manipulate the messenger of God's grace (4.3–4). There are days when we need to remind ourselves that God has blessed us with a treasure far beyond whatever goals we have for ourselves. His gifts are treasures. His gift is grace. His message is worth protecting.

2 Timothy 1.15: "You are aware of the fact that all who are in Asia turned away from me, among whom are Phygelus and Hermogenes."

Phygelus and Hermogenes—one name means a "fugitive," which he became. The other name means "born of Hermes," a false god. Both lived up to their names, instead of living up to the name of Christ.

> It is a sad thing when the only record made of a man—the only evidence which we have that he ever lived at all—is, that he turned away from a friend, or forsook the paths of true religion. And yet, there are many men of whom the only thing to be remembered of them is, that they lived to do wrong. (Barnes, 218)

Here's a question I do not want us to skip over. Ponder this seriously. The first answer might not be the correct one. Honesty is required, maybe even brutal honesty. Here's the question: when our name is mentioned, what do people think? Is it what we want people to think?

Why mention this to Timothy? Obviously, these men did not rekindle their faith by remembering God's grace. Could that happen to Timothy? Could it happen to you? Could it happen to me?

But why mention this to Timothy? Two reasons:

- To forewarn Timothy against following their example
- To get Timothy to empathize with Paul

Examples can be powerful reminders. Paul has already reminded Timothy of their grace-filled bond: Timothy was his son (1.2, 2.1), and Timothy had shed tears of love for his "father" (v. 4). In troublesome times, do we sometimes need to be reminded of important spiritual relationships?

2 Timothy 1.16: "The Lord grant mercy to the house of Onesiphorus, for he often refreshed me and was not ashamed of my chains."

Bad examples can be powerfully effective, but maybe even more so can good examples. Bad examples teach me what not to do. Good examples teach me what to do, plus give encouragement that I can do it.

Timothy did not want to become a spiritual fugitive and deny his inherited name— "son." But a grace-enflamed life is not just negative, keeping us from falling; a grace-led life is also positive, lifting us up to what we can become. Timothy does not need to fail. He can succeed. Why? Because others have, namely, Paul and Onesiphorus, whose name means "profit bearer." Onesiphorus was a man who would live up to his name. Paul "profited" from the "profit bearer." Now, would Paul profit from Timothy? Would the son follow the father?

What had this other Christian done? He refreshed Paul, which meant "originally to cool; to revive by fresh air" (Vincent, 4, 294–295). Therefore, Paul is saying, "Heat yourself up Timothy so you can cool me down!" When had this man refreshed Paul? When Paul had been deserted by others. When Onesiphorus himself might share the same fate. When Timothy needed to rekindle his gift.

It is all so easy to do the right thing when it is not difficult to do the right thing. However, living in the grace of God is doing the right thing when it is not easy, but difficult. It is doing the right thing even though we might suffer when it might cause others to suffer, when we want to run and hide, and when others have already run away. It is doing the right thing whenever we need to live in the grace of God!

2 Timothy 2.1: "You therefore, my son, be strong in the grace that is in Christ Jesus."

Whenever you see a "therefore," see what it is there for! But before we do, notice the tenderness found in the phrase, "my son." There is the emotional attachment again brought out by Paul calling Timothy his son. Literally, it is "child" (*teknon*), which can be used metaphorically to refer to either the student of a teacher or the close, personal, and emotional tie between two people. Both apply rather well here. Sharers in grace . . . what an exhilarating thought! When we need to encourage others to be strong in the grace of God, either because of weakness or upcoming tests, our having a close relationship with them will enable the exhortation to have a greater effect.

Now back to the therefore . . . what is it there for? Paul's encouragement to rekindle Timothy's gift, because of the grace of God, leads the apostle to emphasize that source of strength. If grace is my reason for going on, then I need to emphasize that reason while going on. Therefore, be strong in the grace that is in Christ Jesus. To be strong literally is to "be strengthened inwardly." Is grace only something we receive, or is it also something we use? Remember, the subject is strength in suffering. How was Jesus our example, our grace? All our strength comes from Jesus' grace, but we must use our free will to connect to it.

2 Timothy 2.2: "The things which you have heard from me in the presence of many witnesses, entrust these to faithful men who will be able to teach others also."

Paul is not two-faced in his teaching. What he teaches in one place, he teaches everyplace (1 Cor. 4.17). Methods (i.e., style) might change, but not the message. But why should it? The message is God's glorious grace. The message is about death being abolished. The message is what gets all of us through the day.

Let me ask you a question: when you are needing strength, what can you do to become stronger? Let's remember the context. Paul is trying to encourage Timothy to rekindle his flame. What does Paul do to strengthen Timothy? Within this context, he not only reminds him of God's grace, gives him both good and bad examples, and emphasizes their personal relationship, but now he gives him a specific job to do. This job involves teaching others, which is sharing God's grace. This job includes fellowshiping others. Are you needing strength? Grace is the reply. Grace received. Grace remembered. Grace reciprocated. Grace regenerated. Grace revealed.

In reciprocating God's grace, Timothy is to share and teach others. In doing this, he will entrust [*paratithemi*] the gospel message to others. To entrust means "to set before," whether applied to truth (used of Jesus teaching a parable) or food. After reciprocating God's grace through teaching, God's immortal grace will regenerate in others and continue to spread like a rekindled wild fire. Timothy's gift is as a teacher and preacher. Grace is the strength.

Teaching others is not only a secret to personal growth; it is the secret to church growth. Teach people how to instruct others who will, in turn, teach others the same. A visual illustration would be a mirror held up to another mirror. What is the visual experience? One of unending mirrors. Who are they to teach? Whoever needs teaching. Let us all ask: when was the last time we taught somebody? If it has been a while, how strong are we in the grace of God?

2 Timothy 2.3: "Suffer hardship with me, as a good soldier of Christ Jesus."

If this is what Paul is getting at, why doesn't he just come right out and say so at the beginning? This is not something easy to say, read, or hear. No one wants to suffer. No one wants others to suffer. And yet, ironically, no one wants to suffer alone. Strength is found in grace-sharers sharing grace. Strength is also found in preparation for suffering. We are soldiers, and we are at war, with our greatest weapon being grace. It is both offensive and defensive. Offensively we can use it to save souls. Defensively we can use it to save ourselves from others. Grace, as a weapon, promises us that if we die, we do not die.

Paul now gives us three analogies:

2 Timothy 2.4: "No soldier in active service entangles himself in the affairs of everyday life, so that he may please the one who enlisted him as a soldier."

What are the affairs of everyday life? Whatever they were, Timothy is not to entangle himself. To entangle has been descriptively used of a sheep whose wool had been caught in a fence, which causes us to flinch.

Honesty demands that I admit my uncertainty of what the contextual affairs of everyday life are. But whatever it means, I do not believe the negative command is a call to establish monasteries or to sequester ourselves away from the world. Grace kept is not grace shared. Grace kept is not grace. This is also not a call to celibacy, although marriage itself does bring its own "busyness" (1 Cor. 7.32–35). Maybe the affairs of life are the daily requirements brought on by a job (Acts 18.2–5). Could Paul be asking Timothy to quit his job and devote himself to full-time preaching? Perhaps. That kind of fits the context. After all, Timothy would have to quit his job to come to Paul. But honestly, that interpretation leaves me a little empty. It seems too simplistic. But I wonder if the affairs of everyday life are, instead, just life itself with the daily concerns we all have. What kind of daily concerns could that be? How about fear, worry, doubt, anger, and hate. Everyday life is filled with those entanglements. What has been the theme? God's grace gives us immortal life. Grace defeats fear. Grace rekindles faith. Is there anything more entangling in this life than fear? Is there anything that defeats faith more than fear and its brother doubt? Because of grace, we do not need to be afraid of fear or doubt. Because of grace, we do not need to be afraid of the troubles of this life or doubt God's goodness. Maybe the understanding here is far simpler . . . and far more complicated. Maybe it is time to stop worrying about worry. To stop obsessing about what might happen. To not be afraid. Simple in theory, yet difficult in practice . . . in every day life.

Who is Timothy to please? The gift-giver. The grace-giver. Don't be afraid. Don't be timid, Timothy . . . .

2 Timothy 2.5: "Also if anyone competes as an athlete, he does not win the prize unless he competes according to the rules."

Are there any rules Paul is referring to (1.13, 2.2, 3.15, etc.)? Could Paul be referring to the fact that living a godly life will bring persecution (3.12)? For example, playing by the rules of most sports involves contact—physical, painful, contact. Could this also be a subtle hint to not fail while striving for the prize?

2 Timothy 2.6: "The hard-working farmer ought to be the first to receive his share of the crops."

What is the contextual application? While rightly it could be applied to wages as in 1 Corinthians 9, could the direct application here be God's grace? Maybe Paul could be speaking of Timothy himself as being his (Paul's) wages. But maybe, the context overrules all that and suggests this is an analogy of being strengthened in grace (v. 1) so that Timothy could suffer hardship (v. 3). If I preach grace, I should receive grace from God.

2 Timothy 2.7: "Consider what I say, for the Lord will give you understanding in everything."

Paul is begging Timothy, "Go deeper with my words." What is the crop of grace? "Consider" literally means to put your mind on. It means to "exercise the mind" (Strong, 50). Today we might say, "Put your thinking hat on" or "wrap your mind around this." For us, the word "consider" does not have the strength it apparently once did. For us, to "consider" simply means to weigh our options. "Yes, I considered that possibility, but . . . .," and then we list the reasons for not choosing. Seeing how this same word is used elsewhere in the New Testament gives it a heavier and headier meaning: understood, understand, see, perceive, think. To consider is to "understand," not "maybe choose." Once you and I truly understand what the Lord is saying, is it simply an option?

What Paul is about to say has direct application to everything he has been hoping for in Timothy. Remember how Paul began his letter to Timothy? Remember the dominant theme of life and immortality through the grace of God? Now Paul will show the direct correlation. Is this understanding just intellectual, as in understanding the correct doctrine? Or is it personal and spiritual to where we have to personally admit that something is true before we act on it? Let us understand that grace is first intellectual, but then it should become very personal and spiritual.

Put the three analogies together in Paul's life—and then Timothy's—and we see that he is a soldier who pleased the one who enlisted him, Jesus. He lived according to the rules of the gospel. And get this, he, as a farmer, will reap the crop of his own resurrection. In other words:

> I have fought the good fight [as a soldier], I have finished the course [as an athlete], I have kept the faith; [and as a farmer waits and is rewarded] in the future there is laid up for me the crown of righteousness, which the Lord, the righteous Judge, will award to me on that day; and not only to me, but also to all who have loved His appearing. (2 Timothy 4.7–8)

This crop-resurrection analogy echoes Paul's word to the Corinthians: "But now Christ has been raised from the dead, the first fruits of those who are asleep" (1 Cor. 15.20).

2 Timothy 2.8: "Remember Jesus Christ, risen from the dead, descendant of David, according to my gospel."

That memory rekindles the soul. Memories have a powerful effect. "Remember the Alamo" helped free the independent Texas nation from Mexico. Do you remember your salvation? Does that memory rekindle your faith? It should.

Read this paragraph with a marching cadence, with a shouting voice: no matter what the scene, whether temptation or tribulation, whether in prison with Paul or preaching free like Timothy, let these words echo in our mind and resonate in our soul so that we continually hear that glorious triumphant sound—and that sound will deafen the sirens of Satan—remember Jesus Christ, risen from the dead! And remember, "You too will rise from the dead!"

2 Timothy 2.9: "For which I suffer hardship even to imprisonment as a criminal; but the word of God is not imprisoned."

Can you believe it? Paul, being treated as a common criminal on death row, yet preaching to his captors and fellow captives (Phil. 1). To say that Paul is amazing is an understatement. To say that Paul is amazing is also missing the point. It isn't Paul who is amazing; it is God's amazing grace! Grace made Paul amazing (1 Cor. 15.10). Grace can make us amazing, too, if God gives it to us, and if we use it, and if we give Him the glory, and if we don't think of ourselves as amazing!

Can we think of someone else who had been treated as a common criminal, and preached to his captors and fellow captives! That's right, "Grace Incarnate!"

Another amazing lesson is that grace does not keep us from suffering. We suffer because of grace. And we can endure suffering because of grace. And we can endure it gracefully. Why do bad things happen to good people? Can grace help answer that question? Without getting into a whole other book-load of a topic, let's see what we can learn here about grace, suffering, and good people:

- Jesus suffered. Are we better than He? If Jesus isn't above suffering, who are we to complain? Jesus suffered because people need grace. Maybe that is why I suffer, too. God can use me to show others how to suffer gracefully.

- Jesus suffered because He brought grace. If we bring grace to others, why should we expect not to share His sufferings? The good news is only good news if people accept it. Otherwise, it is bad news because it condemns those who reject it.

- Jesus suffered and showed how grace overshadows the shadow of death. Can I consider suffering a privilege to defeat the devil?

Grace is received because of suffering. Death is the result of sin. Sin brings death to our souls and decay to our bodies. Our souls are forgiven. Our bodies will be resurrected, thanks to grace.

2 Timothy 2.10: "For this reason I endure all things for the sake of those who are chosen, so that they also may obtain the salvation which is in Christ Jesus and with it eternal glory."

Grace can overcome our circumstances if we will be strengthened by it. But did you notice a curious omission and addition? Notice what Paul does not say, "For this reason I endure all things for the sake of those who are chosen, so that . . . I . . . may obtain the salvation." Instead, Paul suffered for others, for them. Just like Christ. And he willingly did so. Just like Christ.

Paul then gives us a "trustworthy statement." This sums up how grace rekindles our gifts, our faith, our souls, our bodies, our lives.

2 Timothy 2.11–13: "It is a trustworthy statement: For if we died with Him, we will also live with Him; if we endure, we will also reign with Him; if we deny Him, He also will deny us; if we are faithless, He remains faithful, for He cannot deny Himself."

Live by grace, and be rekindled. Live because Jesus died. Endure and live forever with the Giver of immortal life. Don't deny Jesus, or He will deny you. And if we do, He remains what we were supposed to be—faithful no matter what.

Paul understood something that escapes so many Christians today. In order to handle our trials, we need to rekindle the inner, spiritual fire so that we might be strong in the grace of Jesus Christ. We need to fight fire with fire! Today, so many let their troubles separate them from God. Paul knew this danger and commends us to fight fire with fire—God's grace!

And remember this: what Jesus asks of us, He already has given. Death is no more real and dangerous than a toy gun. Thanks to grace and the Grace Giver.

Questions

1. In 2 Tim 1.1, what are some possible reasons why Paul reiterated to Timothy his apostleship?

_____

_____

2. For older Christians, what can we learn from Paul's relationship with Timothy and how it relates to grace and rekindling?

_____

_____

3. How does keeping relationships with people who live a grace-led life rekindle us?

_____

_____

4. From 2 Tim, what possibly does Paul's mentioning Timothy's Mother and Grandmother accomplish?

_____

_____

5. What do you think is the purpose of Paul's writing this second letter to Timothy?

_____

_____

6. From 2 Tim. 1.6, how could being reminded of previous spiritual strength be an encouragement to Timothy and to us?

_____

_____

7. In 2 Tim. 1.6, what do the words "kindle afresh" mean?

_____

_____

8. Is "rekindling" only for when our spiritual fires are in danger of dying out? Why?

_____

_____

9. In 2 Tim. 1.7 Paul mentions God not giving a spirit of fear. What are some negative things that fear can bring about within us?

_____

_____

_____

10. How do power, love, and discipline work together in the kindling of our spiritual strength?

_____

_____

11. Since grace is a key aspect to our inner fire, how does grace help us to be unashamed?

12. In 2 Tim. 1.9, how does grace granted in Paul and Timothy by Christ, as well as in us, help to handle life's difficult circumstances?

13. In 2 Tim. 1.10, how does the reiteration of Christ abolishing death connect grace and the rekindling of Timothy's and our inner fires? (Hint: also read Matt. 10.26-28)

14. How does grace make death as real as a toy gun?

15. How can grace and faith work together to encourage us to use our God given gifts for His glory?

16. From 2 Tim. 1.12, how can "believe", "convinced", and "trust" lead us to not be ashamed or filled with fear?

_____

_____

17. How can holding onto the pattern of sound teaching rekindle us in our teaching the gospel? For some clues to spur your thinking, read 2 Tim. 1.13-14, 4.2-5

_____

_____

_____

18. From reading 1 Tim. 6.20; 2 Tim 1.12, 14 and 4.2-5, what could be the "treasure" that needs to be guarded?

_____

_____

_____

19. In 2 Tim 1.15-18, what could be the purpose of Paul mentioning these men to Timothy?

_____

_____

20. Read 2 Tim. 2.1. Is grace only something we receive or is it also something we use?

_____

_____

21. 2 Tim. 2.1-2, How can being strong in grace and teaching the gospel to others create and be a result of a rekindled fire?

22. In 2 Tim. 2.3-7, what could be possible reasons Paul uses these examples?

23. How can 2 Tim. 2.11–13 rekindle Timothy and us?

7

The Grace That Worships

Colossians 3:12-17

An old man lived with his hound-dog, Mace, in a run-down shack on the outskirts of town. Dirt poor, the two of them lived day-to-day. Mace loved chewing grass. That dog would spend the day in the front yard of the house chewing away on the lawn. One day the old man headed into town to work on a plumbing repair job. Inside the house, he reached into his bag for a wrench. To his surprise, he didn't feel it. He dug around in the bag, but there didn't seem to be any wrench. Reality set in. Without a wrench, he couldn't finish the job, and without the pay, he couldn't buy food for that night's supper. The old man headed home, head bowed, and shoulders stooped. But finally, the old shack came into view, and there was Mace in the distance, munching away as usual on the lawn. Kneeling beside the hound, the man began to pet him, and through tear-filled eyes, told the dog that there would be no supper that night and no food for tomorrow. What's more, without money to buy a new wrench, he had no idea what the future held. Then he caught a glimpse of something shining in the grass. When he went over to see what it was, his despair turned in an instant to joy: it was the wrench, right where the dog had been chewing grass! The old man had dropped it on his way out that morning. He ran into the house. Reaching for a stub of pencil and the only piece of paper he had, he wrote a moving tribute to his canine companion. Few people have ever heard these words. But now you are privileged to read the beginning line of his poem, which went: "*A grazing Mace, how sweet the hound that saved a wrench for me.*" (Source unknown probably due to fear of repercussions!)

Pardon me for the pun; I just could not resist. But seriously, why do we sing songs such as "amazing grace, how sweet the sound that saved a wretch like me?" Or an even more encompassing question, "Why do we worship?" Let's begin by looking at three correct answers—ones that will be expanded upon by Colossians 3.

If our first answer as to why we worship and sing is, "we are commanded to," that may be correct, but it is an inadequate and very shallow response. Please don't think I am denigrating obedience. Jesus became to all those who obey Him the source of eternal salvation (Heb. 5.9). "Because we are commanded to" is a proper attitude of submission. But why do we submit? Obeying simply to obey really misses out on the true spiritual nature and holiness of singing and all worship . . . and even obedience itself. Submitting only because we have been commanded defines our relationship with God as solely obligatory and not relational. It needs to be both. Think with me here. As parents, would we want a present on Mother's Day or Father's Day just because our children felt obligated? Even when they obey us, such as doing their chores, don't we want them to have an impulsion that goes beyond obligation? Do we want them to hug us like they do their least favorite relative . . . because they are scolded to?

So back to the question of why do we worship and sing, a second answer is that it glorifies God and teaches about Him, Jesus, and the Holy Spirit. That answer is much more spiritual and very scriptural. We exist to glorify God (Isa. 43.7). And yet, isn't there more to it than that, something more personal? Isn't worship more than simply giving to God what He deserves? I pay my mortgage payment every month because the bank deserves the money, but I sure do not get a thrill out of it.

That brings us to the third answer. Worshipping, and specifically singing, is something that we cannot help but do. Singing is an expression of grace understood (Col. 1.6) and a holiness from within (Col. 2.16–23). We sing because we are filled with Jesus Christ—which is the theme of Colossians (2.9–12). We sing because we are filled with the Spirit (Eph. 5.18–19). We worship because we are compelled from within by grace, a grace that glorifies God, a grace that submits to any and all of God's commands. A grace that worships.

Can we all see how singing, and indeed how all worship is an expression of our innermost feelings, thoughts, and experiences? Singing is as much a part of man as is suffering and joy (Jas. 5.13). People often ask what we can do to have better worship. The answer is we need better worshippers. And better worshippers come from being filled with God's grace.

Now, let's go back to the original question: Why do we worship? Specifically, why do we sing? All of us are familiar with the text in Colossians 3.16, but are we familiar with the context around it? In other words, why did the Holy Spirit put Colossians 3.16 where He did? What surrounds it? Is there anything prior to v. 16 that helps explain v. 16? Could something said before, put v. 16 into perspective? Some Bible versions use bold numbers or lettering to show the beginning of a new paragraph or thought. According to the translators of your Bible, does the Holy Spirit begin a brand new thought in v. 16? Not according to my version (NASB).

The context shows that worshipping God is a delight from within, expressed without. It is an experience born from above, born within our souls. Why do we worship? Grace given, grace received, grace experienced, grace appreciated, grace motivated. Motivation can make all the difference in this world—and the next.

A farmer was driving his pickup with his dog in the seat next to him and a horse trailer in tow behind him. On a dangerous curve, he was forced off the road by a large truck. A highway patrolman happened upon the accident and quickly assessed the damages. Seeing the dog and horse suffering, the patrolman pulled out his revolver and put them out of their misery. He then walked over to the farmer and asked, "How are you doing?" The farmer looked at the smoking pistol, dead animals, and then quickly replied, "I've never felt better!"

Motivation changes our attitudes.

During World War II, the U.S. government discovered its parachutes failed to open 5 percent of the time. Clearly, nothing less than zero defects was an acceptable level of quality. The problem was solved by requiring parachute packers and inspectors to occasionally put on one of their products and jump out of a plane.

Motivation changes our actions.

Attitudes and actions. The next section of this chapter will focus on attitudes. The last section will dwell on attitudes and actions of worship, looking closely at Colossians 3:16.

GRACE MOTIVATED ATTITUDES: TOOLS AND TECHNIQUES

Colossians 3.12–13: "So, as those who have been chosen of God, holy and beloved, put on a heart of compassion, kindness, humility, gentleness and patience; bearing with one another, and forgiving each other, whoever has a complaint against anyone; just as the Lord forgave you, so also should you."

As Christians, we have a unique set of motivational tools and techniques. Read the scripture above once more if you need reminding. They can be looked at in two ways:

Who We Are:	What God Did:
Chosen of God	God Chose Us
Holy	Made Us Holy
Beloved	Loved Us
Forgiven	Forgave Us

Each of these is connected to God's grace, aren't they? It may be unnecessary, but notice that these motivations cannot be called, "what we did." That's why it is grace! The reason I am motivated to worship and behave godly with others is because of my God, who behaves godly with me. God's grace is what motivates and moves me.

Motive is the beginning place for all attitudes and actions. "For as he thinks within himself, so he is" (Prov. 23.7). Motive is what "moves" us to do something. In fact, "motive" and "motor" are from the same Latin word, *movere,* to move. Motive is an inward prompting or impulse, which moves a person to do what he does. It is often desire or fear or another emotion (another cognate of motive) that influences a person's choices.

While studying philosophy in a university, I learned of one man's philosophy regarding motivation. There is only one motive, according to this philosopher, and that is selfishness. Even the seemingly selfless acts of benevolence are only done to keep ourselves from feeling guilty. A more pessimistic, cynical, despondent life-philosophy does not exist. What a blasphemous thought! Why is it blasphemous? Because my motive of love for God is an imitation of Divine love—a love that gives grace. God is not motivated by selfishness.

Again, better worship requires better worshippers—grace-filled worshippers.

GRACE CLOTHES NOT GRAVE CLOTHES

Colossians 3.12, 14: "So, as those who have been chosen of God, holy and beloved, put on a heart of compassion, kindness, humility, gentleness and patience. Beyond all these things put on love, which is the perfect bond of unity."

When we "go to church," what do we wear? Do we put on our "Sunday best"? What we put on to go to church should already have been put on before we got dressed to go to church. What we put on is not supposed to be taken off. Now that I have confounded you with my wisdom, what do we put on? Warren Wiersbe described what we put on as being our "grace clothes," and what we take off are our "grave clothes" (Wiersbe, 111).

What we put on is a wonderful example of how to help new Christians succeed. Colossians 2 teaches us a sure-fire method of failure—holiness from the outside-in and man-made traditions and rules. Grace leads to holiness from the inside-out. Grace leads to holiness because Christ is living within us.

Trying to live a grace-filled life requires changes. With what do we replace our old bad habits? Not new habits or traditions, because habits and traditions can be mechanical, including religious habits and traditions. We need to fill our lives with Christ and His grace. Succeeding in our daily life leads to succeeding in our worship life because we are to worship daily with our lives (Rom. 12.1–2). This doesn't mean everything I do is worship—I don't worship God by eating Krispy Kreme doughnuts, although I dearly enjoy eating them. But it does mean that my life itself is a worship service. Remember, better worship requires better worshippers. Better worshippers are motivated by grace.

Psychologists call the method in Colossians three "replacement therapy." More biblically, it is holiness from the inside-out. New Christians need to replace their old sinful habits, thoughts, and ways, not through man-made applications, but through the new man. This leads to and involves worship and grace. This leads to and involves worship with others who are wearing their grace clothes.

There is a divine emphasis on our human relationships. These relationships with one another are directly related to our relationship with God. Worship is not just an act of solitude, although it can be done alone. It is an expression of God's relationship with us and our relationship with others who are in the same relationship with God. It is an expression of God's shared grace, sharing with one another in expressing grace.

People who claim, "I don't need to go to church because I can worship God anywhere," are right . . . and wrong. Yes, we can worship God anywhere, but our worship experience is enhanced by our personal experience with others who have put on grace.

Grace received removes our grave clothes, allowing us to worship God and transcend this world. Worshipping God is as close to being caught up into paradise as we will get before we forever remove our grave clothes in the resurrection. In order to remove sin, we apply the blood of Jesus. That's grace. In order to remove the love of sin, which is worldliness, we replace it with the love of God, which is the love of righteousness. That is also grace. And that is a lifetime process.

Speaking of removing and replacing, how do you plant trees, flowers, and bushes? You dig a hole (remove) and put the plant in the hole (replace). Although that is not a thorough explanation, it will suffice, especially from a city boy like me. Too many people are planting Jesus into their lives in totally useless ways. That's why their worship is lacking.

Some people dig the hole and forget to plant the flowers. This is like the man who was demon-possessed (Matt. 12.43-45). He did not fill his inner emptiness with God so that there would be no room for the demons. And they returned. We cannot worship God in our life and with our life, without God in our life.

Others just throw the plant on the ground. They never dig the world out of themselves to make room for Jesus and His love and righteousness. We cannot worship God if we are worshipping ourselves.

Still, others start the process right, digging, watering, and fertilizing, only to neglect themselves once they think they are established. We cannot worship God if we do not continue to grow in the grace and knowledge of our Lord Jesus Christ (2 Pet. 3.18).

Another analogy is cancer surgery, which not only includes cutting out the cancerous tissue but also repairing and closing the wound. And remember, doctors not only have to repair as best they can the damage done by the cancer, but also the damage they caused by removing the cancer. So what are our "grace clothes"? What is it that we are to "put on"?

- Heart (lit., bowels) of compassion
- Kindness (2 Samuel 9.3)
- Humility (same word as in Col, 2.18,23)
- Gentleness (i.e., meekness)—used to describe a soothing wind, a healing medicine, and a "broken" horse
- Patience (i.e., toward others—same word as in Col. 1.11)
- Love (v. 14)

Reflect on our grace clothes, and ponder whether or not true worship is easy. Singing is as easy as opening our mouth. Worshipping is as hard as opening our heart. Just living these are worship! Again, can we see that in order to have better worship, we need better worshippers?

GRACE MOTIVATED ACTIONS
WORSHIP—FORGIVING ONE ANOTHER

Colossians 3.13: "Bearing with one another, and forgiving each other, whoever has a complaint against anyone; just as the Lord forgave you, so also should you."

I can't say the next point is exactly what the Holy Spirit had in mind, but I do wonder why He first said to "bear with one another" before saying, "forgive one another." I wonder if the point is that sometimes we must first psychologically put up with some people before we can emotionally forgive them. I do know this—people often worship with others where there is a whole lot of bearing with one another going on.

Why put forgiveness in a section involving worship? Two brothers, both Christians, went into business together. The business went bad. They sat on opposite sides of the church building, not talking to each other for 20 years. Did they worship together when they worshipped? Eventually, the relationship was healed. Forgiveness is eternally tied to worship. How can we go into the presence of God when we don't allow others in our own presence?

> Matthew 5.23–24: Therefore if you are presenting your offering at the altar, and there remember that your brother has something against you, leave your offering there before the altar and go; first be reconciled to your brother, and then come and present your offering.

So how do we forgive more easily? Grace. Remember, we are to forgive just as the Lord forgave us. We need to take our own sin more seriously, which is the only way to truly appreciate our forgiveness and God's grace. Then we can forgive more easily. Worship is far more horizontal than we sometimes realize. What God does for us leads to what we do for others and with others.

Forgiveness is hard, which is why we need grace clothes. On forgiving one another, Vincent comments that "one another is better translated yourselves, emphasizing the fact that they are all members of Christ's body—everyone members one of another – so that, in forgiving each other they forgive themselves" (Vol. 3, 505). Whether that is true or not, I do know that forgiving is giving a gift for others and for yourself.

The actions of bearing with and forgiving one another make for better worship because we become better worshippers. When we receive grace, we give grace, and then we worship in grace.

WORSHIP—PEACE WITHIN

Colossians 3.15–17: "Let the peace of Christ rule in your hearts, to which indeed you were called in one body; and be thankful. Let the word of Christ richly dwell within you, with all wisdom teaching and admonishing one another with psalms and hymns and spiritual songs, singing with thankfulness in your hearts to God. Whatever you do in word or deed, do all in the name of the Lord Jesus, giving thanks through Him to God the Father."

The peace of Christ within (v. 15), the word of Christ within (v. 16), the name of the Lord Jesus in all things (v. 17). Peace comes from receiving God's grace. Receiving God's grace leads to letting His word live within me. Having the word of Christ within, leads to total submission to His will and doing what He wants and only what He wants. We've got a long way to go, don't we?

What God has done by replacing grave clothes with grace clothes should lead us to being peaceful and thankful within and sharing with others as one body. We should gracefully worship our Lord and Savior with others who are spiritually one with us—the one body of Christ. We should gracefully worship our Lord and Savior with others who are peaceful and thankful within.

If we are living in spiritual peace, being thankful to Jesus, letting His word richly dwell within us, and doing everything because of Him, we have succeeded in becoming holy from the inside out. Grace lives within. And it is this grace-filled holiness that leads us to singing and worshipping. This holiness comes from accepting and living in God's grace. That's why we worship. We are filled with and living in God's grace.

PERRY HALL

WORSHIP—WHY DO WE SING?

Colossians 1.16: (J. B. Lightfoot, expanded paraphrase): "Let the inspiring word of Christ dwell in your hearts, enriching you with its boundless wealth and endowing you with all wisdom. Teach and admonish one another with psalms, with hymns of praise, with spiritual songs of all kinds. Only let them be pervaded with grace from heaven. Sing to God in your hearts and not with your lips only."

The phrase, "the word of Christ," is used here because Paul's purpose in writing this epistle is to exalt Christ against gnostic tenets (1.13–20, 2.8–10), which included self-illumination. Paul says that the word of Christ educates. Just as the epistle celebrates Christ, so does our worship . . . and our lives. When we worship, we educate ourselves and those around us.

The word of Christ expresses itself in psalms, hymns, and spiritual songs. The word of Christ is the gospel—grace—whether we understand it as doctrine from Christ or doctrine about Christ. It is no more right to sing a lie than it is to preach a lie since we are supposed to sing the word of Christ. How careful are we about what we sing?

Let's not forget the wonderful example the Holy Spirit reserved for us in Colossians 1.15–20. A modern-day equivalent to such an exalted hymn is, Immortal, Invisible, God Only Wise (Walter Chalmers Smith, 1867). Although I prefer many of the more modern hymns, they usually are not as deep and exalted as this more ancient one.

Immortal, Invisible, God Only Wise

Immortal, invisible, God only wise,
In light inaccessible hid from our eyes,
Most blessed most glorious, the Ancient of Days,
Almighty, victorious, Thy great name we praise.

Unresting, unhasting, and silent as light,
Nor wanting, nor wasting, Thou rulest in might;
Thy justice like mountains high soaring above
Thy clouds, which are fountains of goodness and love.

> To all, life Thou givest, to both great and small;
> In all life Thou livest, the true life of all;
> We blossom and flourish as leaves on the tree,
> And wither and perish—but naught changeth Thee.
>
> Great Father of glory, pure Father of light,
> Thine angels adore Thee, all veiling their sight;
> All praise we would render: O help us to see
> 'Tis only the splendor of light hideth Thee.

That song might not be as easy to sing as Jesus Loves Me, or as musically beautiful as many modern ones are, but it is a powerful teaching song.

What is a psalm? What is a hymn? What is a spiritual song? What is our motivation for singing them? Remember, at the beginning, we talked about how motivations move us.

> One Sunday, a preacher told the congregation that the church needed some extra money and asked the people to prayerfully consider giving a little extra in the offering plate. He said that whoever gave the most would be able to pick out three hymns.
>
> After the offering plates were passed, the preacher glanced down and noticed that someone had placed a $1,000 check in the offering. He was so excited that he immediately shared his joy with his congregation and said he'd like to personally thank the person who placed the money in the plate.
>
> A very quiet, elderly, saintly lady all the way in the back shyly raised her hand. The preacher asked her to come to the front. Slowly she made her way to the preacher. He told her how wonderful it was that she gave so much, and in thanksgiving asked her to pick out three hymns. Her eyes brightened as she looked over the congregation, pointed to the three most handsome men in the building, and said, "I'll take him, and him, and him."

Would our worship be more energetic if the motivation was temporal? If our motivation is praise from others because God blessed us with a beautiful voice, how are we any different than that dear old woman wanting the three "hims?"

We are to sing psalms, hymns, and spiritual songs. We are to sing the word of Christ. Usually, we restrict our application of the phrase, word of Christ/God/Lord, to the inspired writings in the Bible. And to a great degree that is proper and scriptural. Only the Bible contains the direct words of God. However, the word of Christ also finds itself embodied in humanly written songs when these express Biblical truths. These songs have been called "songs of human composition" as opposed to the songs directly composed by inspiration, such as are found in Psalms. Ironically, many commonly accepted songs of human composition were once new, radical, and rejected. Today they are orthodox and old fashioned.

The Holy Spirit uses three different words to describe what we are to sing. The first is psalms (*psalmos*). While this might obviously describe songs from the Old Testament songbook known as Psalms—and historically, some groups will only sing these Psalms—that might be restricting the meaning too far.

The term psalm occurs in two different ways in the New Testament. The first is obviously referring to the book of Psalms (Luke 20.42), which is the specific use of that term. However, in looking at 1 Corinthians 14.26 and other passages, it is possible that the term is also used generally to simply mean "religious song." In our text here, it is probable that the term psalm is not meant to be specific, but rather only generic. I would say this for two reasons:

First, when "the Psalms" is referred to, it is very specific that is what is being spoken of (i.e., Acts 1.20). The language in both Colossians 3.16 and Ephesians 5.19 is very generic— "psalms." Apparently, most translators agree because they do not capitalize the word as a proper noun.

Second, not all of the OT Psalms would be appropriate for us to sing today:

- Psalm 68.29: "Because of Your temple at Jerusalem kings will bring gifts to You."
- Psalm 138.2: "I will bow down toward Your holy temple and give thanks to Your name for Your lovingkindness and Your truth; for You have magnified Your word according to all Your name.
- Psalm 51.19: Then You will delight in righteous sacrifices, in burnt offering and whole burnt offering; then young bulls will be offered on Your altar.

- Psalm 58.6: O God, shatter their teeth in their mouth; break out the fangs of the young lions, O LORD.
- Psalm 137.9: How blessed will be the one who seizes and dashes your little ones against the rock.

The next word is hymns (*humnos*). If there is a distinct meaning in the three words—and not all scholars agree that there is—then hymns are songs that glorify and praise God. Some songs are sung "to" one another, such as, *Rescue the Perishing*. While that song might be in a "hymn book," that song is not technically a hymn. Hymns are not only directed to God, they are filled with praise to Him as God.

The third word is actually two: spiritual (*pneumatikos*) songs (*ode*)—songs not of a carnal nature. This is just a specific type of song that it is spiritual, but other than that, it appears to be the most generic of the three words.

Different people have observed that the most powerful people in a nation are not the lawmakers, but the songwriters— "a successful Christian life involves attention to three books: God's Book, the bible; the pocketbook; and the hymnbook." (Wiersbe, 119) I would like to amend that observation and say that the most powerful people in a nation are those filled with grace, whether writing or singing psalms, hymns, and spiritual songs.

Plato deemed music so powerful he thought the state should control it. How powerful is music? Have you ever caught yourself unwittingly singing a beer commercial? It would do us all well if we actually memorized our favorite spiritual songs.

WORSHIP—WHO ARE TO SING?

People arguing over the scripturalness of solos, duets, choirs, and such really miss the point—on both sides. Whether we believe such arrangements are scriptural or not, please notice the Holy Spirit's language: "Let the word of Christ richly dwell within you." If singing is an expression of the grace clothes we have put on, then who should sing? Verses 1–15 describes the ones who should sing. Singing is something grace-filled people have to do! Singing because of grace is like hitting your thumb with a nail—you can't help but to let it all out! And admittedly, some people sing like they have hit their thumb

. . . but we won't go there. Singing is not entertainment—it is an expression of what's inside. It is an expression of what we have received.

Let's expand the application of the word of Christ living within us. If the word of Christ dwells within us and we don't sing that word, are we fulfilling the Holy Spirit's motivation for having that word within? But more importantly, are we truly filled?

WORSHIP—WHO ARE TO LISTEN?

All are to listen to one another, teach, and admonish through song. The same people who are to sing to one another are to bear with one another and forgive one another (v. 13). These are the people who are to teach and admonish. I sometimes wonder if we are so busy singing and listening to ourselves that we do not actually listen to what others are singing to us? That's one reason I like to face others when I sing . . . instead of facing the back of their heads.

A lady filled with the word of Christ fulfilled this command when she sung to a new Christian whom she was counseling concerning abuse. She sang, *Do You Know My Jesus*. Singing and worship are far more than what takes place in the assembly. It also takes place outside the assembly. But most importantly, whether in or out of the assembly, singing and worship takes place within us, by us, for us, for others, and to God.

Who else listens? God. God is the recipient of our praise (see the meaning of "hymn"). And God is the audience of our praise. Why? Because of the reason we sing, which is grace. However, we should always remember that God is involved in our singing. Thankfully, He does not listen with a human ear, painfully shrieking when we are off-key. In fact, I have a theory. God actually enjoys hearing people sing off-key because there is no doubt that they are not singing for their own glory. Does that mean God does not care how our singing sounds? The answer is an unequivocal yes . . . and no. God couldn't care less how well we can carry a tune but rather how we carry our heart. God has always required and deserved our best. When we consider the motivation of grace, shouldn't we be moved to offering the best, even if it means needing to work hard to offer our best?

WORSHIP—HOW ARE WE TO SING?

First, sing wisely—with all wisdom (*sophia*). Words are to fit the moment. Proverbs 25.11: "Like apples of gold in settings of silver is a word spoken in right circumstances." *Oh, Why Not Tonight* sung on Sunday morning? A person might be thinking of responding that morning to God's grace, and we sing *Oh, Why Not Tonight*? What are we trying to do, talk them out of it?

Do we understand the words we are using? Old fashioned words such as "Ebenezer stone" are lost on today's crowd. So if there is a song with content you do not understand, look up the meaning! There is also another danger of focusing so much on the musical aspect that we don't consider the words. Have you ever sung a song and then later read the words and only then have it dawn on you what you had been singing? For example, what is the song, *I'll Be Somewhere Listening* about? Did you know that you are singing about when you will be in the grave listening for the resurrection call? What a beautiful concept found in that song. But like many concepts, it can be lost if time is not taken to understand the words being sung.

Second, sing heartfully (if that's not a real word, it should be)—singing with thankfulness in your hearts (*kardia*). I sing spiritual songs a cappella for theological reasons, but I would like to suggest a very practical reason: it is easier to hear the heart.

> This word [of Christ – PDH] is to have its settled abode in the hearts of Christians so that there is a submission to its demands. (Carson, 90)

Here is a comment on a similar expression found in Philippians 1.7–8:

> "I have you in my heart" means more in the Greek than it does in the English; for in the Greek the heart is not the seat of the affections, these are located in the viscera (v. 8). The heart is the seat of the personality with its mind, feeling, and will, notably the latter. Paul is not merely holding the Philippians dear, he is holding them, we may say, as part of himself, his mind and his will ever being concerned about them." (Lenski, VIII, 712)

As Paul made believers part of himself, we also make the word of Christ part of ourselves, so much so that when we sing, we are singing in our hearts.

WORSHIP—WHY SHOULD WE SING?

Ahh, here we come to the most important question—why! And there are many "whys."

We sing to glorify Christ. Although this is not directly expressed, the tenor of the whole epistle is explained by the exclusive use of the phrase, "word of Christ." Our singing is praise to Christ as God. This is an indirect, secondary argument for the divinity and incarnation of Christ. Colossians 1.15–20 exalts Christ. Many scholars believe it to be an early hymn.

We sing because the word of Christ richly dwells in us. Let's look at this verse by asking a question. What will happen if you "Let the word of Christ richly dwell within you?" I believe it is answered by the following clause: you will, with all wisdom, teach and admonish one another. In other words, we can't help but sing. Look at the word dwell (*enoikeo*)—it means to "to inhabit" (Strong, 29). It is from *oikeo*, "to occupy a house, i.e., reside" plus *en* (Strong, 51). The word of Christ should be housed in me, in my heart. "But Paul's command to let Christ's word 'dwell' (v. 16) in them means simply to let "Christ's word 'live in' them" (Songer, 110). This means that Christ—and His words—is "to make one's home, to be at home" (Robertson, IV, 505) in us. We become a sanctuary of song. *Sanctuary* by John W. Thompson (v. 1; vv. 2–3, unknown) is one of my favorite modern songs:

1. O Lord, prepare me to be a sanctuary, pure and holy, tried, and true. With thanksgiving, I'll be a living sanctuary for You.

2. It was You, Lord, who gave the Savior, heart and soul, Lord, to every man. It is You, Lord, who knows my weakness, You refine me with Thine own hand.

3. Lead me, O Lord, thru temptation, You refine me from within. Fill our hearts with Your Holy Spirit, and take all our sins away.

Why else do we sing and worship?

We sing so that we can teach (*didasko*) and admonish (*noutheteo*). These are just positive and negative sides of the same thing. We are to sing the word of Christ. Why do that? For the same reason we preach—Colossians 1.28:

"We proclaim Him, admonishing every man and teaching every man with all wisdom, so that we may present every man complete in Christ."

Singing helps complete us, probably in more ways than we know. Teaching and admonishing requires words. That might sound simplistic, but it might just be radical. "Christian music" today emphasizes the mechanical far more than the instructional. Christian music should instruct as much as reading the word instructs, hearing a sermon instructs, or being in a Bible class instructs.

Here is my favorite part—we sing because we have received God's grace/singing with thankfulness (lit., in His grace). Personally, I think "thankfulness" is a bad translation for *charisi*. Although I'm admittedly not a Greek scholar, it is my opinion that *charis* should be translated "grace," as many translations do. Surely, grace includes thankfulness, but the word thankfulness does not tell us why we are thankful. Grace includes thankfulness, but thankfulness does not necessarily include grace.

> Our singing must be with grace. This does not mean "singing in a gracious way," but singing because we have God's grace in our hearts. It takes grace to sing when we are in pain, or when circumstances seem to be against us. It certainly took grace for Paul and Silas to sing in that Philippian prison (Acts 16:22-25). Our singing must not be a display of fleshly talent; it must be a demonstration of the grace of God in our hearts." (Wiersbe, 119)
>
> The definite article seems to exclude all lower senses of (*charis*) here, such as "acceptable," "sweetness" (see iv.6). The interpretation "with gratitude," if otherwise tenable (comp.1 Cor. x.30), seems inappropriate here because the idea of thanksgiving is introduced in the following verse." (Lightfoot, 226)

If Paul had meant thankfulness, he could have repeated a form of the same basic word (*eucharistos* in v.15). At first glance, the phrase with thankfulness might convey how we are to sing. After further investigation, I am inclined to believe it is why we are to sing.

Worship and singing are to be amazing actions of grace. We began with a parody of *Amazing Grace*. Here is the story behind what some feel is the most beloved hymn of all time:

It was not uncommon, in eighteenth-century England, for a boy to spend several uninspiring months in boarding school and then head out to sea.

That's how it happened for John. When John was eleven, his father—a master of a ship in the Mediterranean trade—took the boy on board.

This early training provided excellent groundwork for John's next major seafaring experience, impressment into the British Navy.

Yet what John had gained from his father's knowledge of sailing, he had lost in discipline. John was soon arrested for desertion, publicly flogged, and demoted to common sailor.

Still in his teens, John received permission to sail on the H.M.S. Harwich, bound for the African coast. By now, the unsettled and impatient youth was emerging as the rotten apple in the barrel.

Mocking authority, he chose his friends unwisely and "sank to the depths of vice."

In Africa, John fell into the service of a slave dealer. Slave trade began to fascinate John as a lucrative livelihood, but before he knew it, he was put to work on the dealer's plantation laboring with the other slaves.

"At twenty-one, John escaped. Hopping an outbound ship called the Greyhound, he presently returned to the depravity of his teens.

"Associating with the lowest of crew members, John ridiculed the upright seamen in his company, ridiculed the ship's captain—even ridiculed a book he had found on board. A book entitled The Imitation of Christ. Clearly, he remembered joking about that book one bright afternoon.

That night the Greyhound sailed into a violent storm. John awakened to discover his cabin filled with seawater. The ship's side had caved in, and the Greyhound was going down. The Greyhound had sailed into high seas; her side collapsed in the turbulence.

Ordinarily, such damage would send a ship to the bottom within a few minutes. In this case, the Greyhound's buoyant cargo bought a few hours of precious time.

After nine hours at the pumps, John overheard a desperate remark from one of the crew. They were all goners, he said.

And almost in answer, John—unwittingly and for the first time in his life—prayed. "If this will not do, the Lord have mercy on us!"

The record shows that the Greyhound did not go down.

Although one might have expected John's prayer of emergency to be quickly forgotten, it was remembered unto his death. Each year he observed the anniversary of that most significant incident with prayer and fasting. In a very real sense, he observed it throughout each remaining day of his life.

For John retired from the sea to become a minister. Also a writer of verse.

And the immortal words of a bad boy turned good, the distant reflection of an event long past, are celebrated to this day:

> Amazing grace! How sweet the sound,
> That saved a wretch like me!
> I once was lost, but now am found,
> Was blind, but now I see.

John was John Newton. And now you know The Rest of the Story. (Paul Aurandt, 49–50)

Why do we sing? The word of Christ lyrically and musically bursts from our souls, expressing the grace we have received from God. We are a living sanctuary singing grace. We are a singing sanctuary abounding in grace. We are a holy sanctuary of God. That's why we sing! That's why we worship! Amazing grace how sweet the sound, that saved a wretch like me.

Questions

1. Why do we sing and worship?

_____

_____

_____

_____

2. What do we need to have better worship?

_____

_____

3. How can we answer why we worship by grace? Grace _____, grace _____, grace _____, grace _____, and grace _____.

4. In Col. 3.12-13 list who we are and what God did:

_____

_____

5. How does Col. 3 teach holiness from the inside out?

_____

_____

6. How could having put on our "grace clothes", the things we are to put on listed in Col. 3.12-14, enhance our worship together?

_____

_____

7. In Col 3.13, could there be a deep connection between bearing and forgiving one another? Why?

_____

_____

_____

8. How is grace and forgiveness connected to worship? Col 3.13, Matt 5.23-24

_____

_____

_____

9. In Col. 3.15-17, summarize how we become peaceful and thankful: the _____ of Christ, the _____ of Christ, and the _____ of Lord Jesus in all things.

10. In Col. 3.16, what is the likely meaning of:
Psalm _____
Hymn _____
Spiritual Songs _____

11. How powerful are songs as teaching tools?

_____

12. According to Col. 3.1-16, who is to sing?

_____

_____

_____

13. According to Col. 3.1-16, who is to listen to singing?

_____

_____

14. Is there importance in the choice of what we sing and when it is sung?

_____

_____

15. From Col. 3.16, if the word of Christ is dwelling richly within us, what should follow?

_____

_____

16. Why do we sing?

_____

_____

Conclusion

Grace. The Originator and Giver of Grace provides daily beyond the initial purpose and need. As we grow in the grace and knowledge of our Lord Jesus Christ, the paradoxes of Christianity are lived and discovered and relived and rediscovered. Grace is much more than how we are spiritually alive. It is how we survive. It is how we thrive.

The Holy Spirit has shined God's divine light revealing exciting truths and revealing spiritual tools by revealing the manifold grace of God. When light shines through a diamond, the diamond becomes a prism exposing light's hidden wonders. Using God's revelation, a prism-like rainbow reveals the various wonders of grace needed every day. This is a gift the Son of God continues to give. This is a gift the man of God continues to need.

So as we conclude this journey together, let me ask, did you get surprised by grace? If so, can you through grace, confidently approach Christ to receive His all-sufficient grace? Our boldness and confidence come from being insufficient individually and, therefore, sufficient divinely. Do you feel obligated by grace to keep being motivated by grace? Our ability to morally live and sacrificially give depends upon it. Are you fired up by grace because you better understand grace? Our inward strength comes from a personal relationship with Jesus based upon knowing and believing who He is and who He is to us. If you feel confident, sufficient, obligated, motivated, rekindled, and willing to walk worthy with Jesus, then live a life of grace-filled worship. Live a life of grace-revealed service. Live a life hoping, believing, and knowing that yes, "grace does that!"

Bibliography

Aurandt, Paul. 1980. More of Paul Harvey's The Rest of the Story. New York: Bantam Books.

Barber, Wayne. June 2001. Consequences of Preaching the Gospel. Pulpit Helps, 12.

Barclay, William. 1976. The Letter to the Hebrews. Philadelphia: The Westminster Press.

Barnes, Albert. 1981. Notes on the New Testament Explanatory and Practical, 2 Timothy. Grand Rapids, MI: Baker Book House.

Baxter, J. Sidlow. 1970. The Strategic Grasp of the Bible. Grand Rapids, MI: Zondervan Publishing House.

Bruce, F. F. April–June 1984. The "Christ Hymn" of Colossians 1.15–20. Bibliotheca Sacra, 141(562). Electronic edition by Galaxie Software, 1999, via TheoCenTric.

Brueggemann, Walter. 1982. Genesis, Interpretation, A Bible Commentary for Teaching and Preaching. Atlanta: John Knox Press.

Brumback, Carl. 1959. God In Three Persons. Cleveland TN: Pathway Press.

Carson, H. M. 1984. Colossians and Philemon. Grand Rapids, MI: William B. Eerdmans Publishing Company.

Coffman, James Burton. 1973. Commentary on Romans. Austin, TX: Firm Foundation Publishing House.

Earles, Brent. 1987. The Gospels for Graduates. Grand Rapids, MI: Baker Book House.

Everest, Quinton J. 1975, Messages From Romans, volume II. South Bend, IN: Your Worship Hour, Inc.

Hodges, Charles. 1980. An Exposition of the Second Epistle to the Corinthians. Grand Rapids, MI: Baker Book House.

International Standard Bible Encyclopedia. E-Sword version 8.0.5, Rick Myers.

Kittel, G., Friedrich, G., & Bromiley, G. W. 1995, c1985. Theological dictionary of the New Testament. Translation of: Theologisches Worterbuch zum Neuen Testament. Grand Rapids, MI.: W.B. Eerdmans.

Leithart, Peter. www.leithart.com

Lenski, R. C. H. 1946. The Interpretation of St. Paul's First and Second Epistle to the Corinthians. Columbus, OH: Wartburg Press.

_____. 1946. The Interpretation of St. Paul's Epistles to the Galatians to the Ephesians and to the Philippians. Columbus, OH: Wartburg Press.

Lightfoot, J. B. 1982. St. Paul's Epistles to the Colossians and to Philemon, A Revised Text with Introduction, Notes and Dissertations. Lynn, MA: Hendrickson Publishers.

Martin, Ralph P. 1974. Worship In the Early Church. Grand Rapids MI: William B. Eerdman's Publishing Company.

McGuiggan, Jim. 1982. The Book of Romans. Lubbock, TX: Montex Publishing Company.

Meyer, H. A. W. 1983. Critical and Exegetical Handbook to the Epistles. Peabody, MA: Hendrickson Publishers.

Moore, James W. May 1994. Healing Where It Hurts. Dynamic Preaching, IX(5), 6–7.

O'Connor, Elizabeth. 1987. Cry Pain, Cry Hope, Thresholds to Purpose. Waco, TX: Word Books Publisher.

Packer, J. I. Knowing God. 1973. Downers Grove, IL: Intervarsity Press.

Parablius. March 1988. Man Suffers From Rebel Body Parts. 5(3), 9.

Robertson, Archibald Thomas. 1930. Word Pictures in the New Testament, volumes IV, V. Nashville, TN: Broadman Press.

Songer, Harold S. 1973. *Colossians: Christ Above All.* Nashville, TN: Convention Press.

Spain, Carl. 1970. *The Letters of Paul to Timothy and Titus.* Austin, TX: Sweet Publishing Company.

Stern, David H. 1999. *Jewish New Testament Commentary.* Clarksville, MD: Jewish New Testament Publications.

Strong, James. 1980. *The Exhaustive Concordance of the Bible.* Nashville, TN: Abingdon.

Tasker, R. V. G. 1983. *2 Corinthians.* Grand Rapids, MI: William B. Eerdmans Publishing Company.

Thayer, Joseph Henry. 1988. *A Greek-English Lexicon of the New Testament.* Grand Rapids, MI: Baker Book House.

Vincent, Marvin R. 1888. *Word Studies of the New Testament,* volume III. McLean, VA: MacDonald Publishing Company.

Vine, W. E. 1940. *A Comprehensive Dictionary of the Original Greek Words with their Precise Meanings for English Readers.* McLean, VA: MacDonald Publishing Company.

Wiersbe, Warren W. 1984. *Be Complete.* Wheaton, IL: Victor Books. Wuest, K. S. (1997, c1984).

Wuest's word studies from the Greek New Testament : For the English reader (Col 1.14–15). Grand Rapids: Eerdmans. Logos.com

Yancey, Philip. 1997. *What's So Amazing About Grace?* Grand Rapids, MI: Zondervan Publishing House.

Acknowledgements

It seems that every book published nowadays has an Acknowledgement Page. Personally, I read them, though I do not know how many do. This type of page is dedicated to people such as Kenny "Tack" Chumbley (my editor) and Kevin Gillins and Brent Kercheville who made helpful suggestions. It is also proper to mention the Boca Raton church of Christ where I preached these lessons many years ago. And of course authors are supposed to acknowledge all the people who helped in some fashion or manner, especially our wives who put up with us while writing.

It wasn't until I wrote a book that I truly understood the purpose of such an page. Yes, it is humbling to admit all the people who helped produce the book that carries just one name—the author's. But there is another purpose too: to beg these same people to help with the next one by putting their names in the first one!

To my wife, Janet, you are the most amazing woman I know. What is more amazing is that you continue to believe in me. I have always said you are the only reason people take me seriously; because if you think I am worth something, then others believe in me because they believe in you.

To my daughters, Rachel and Ashley, you along with your mother, gave me encouragement when doubt began to encroach. To my sons, Rick and Ken, you gave me relief from work with baseball, football and basketball, a needed respite.

And finally, to my other sons, Tashad and Rashad. Always know that you are here with me every day in my heart.

www.ingramcontent.com/pod-product-compliance
Lightning Source LLC
Chambersburg PA
CBHW030108240426
43661CB00031B/1335/J